The Belle of the Belfast City
and
Did You Hear The One About The Irishman . . . ?

Christina Reid's work belongs to the new vein of 'flinty documentary' (Michael Coveny, *Financial Times*) that is revitalizing Northern Irish theatre. The community she describes is her own and she has a deep understanding of the traditions, loyalties and affections that guide the city's inhabitants.

Of her first play **Tea in a China Cup** (winner of the Thames TV Award 1983) the *Irish Times* wrote: 'A new talent, acutely perceptive and gently voiced, has emerged in Northern Irish theatre . . . From a succession of small, revelatory incidents a tapestry of humour, prejudice, affection, courage and pretence is woven over a ground of sympathy.'

Joyriders, Christina Reid's second play about the hard-won victories and daily degradations of Belfast youth, was also highly acclaimed: 'What makes **Joyriders** so impressive is the way that it suggests the extent to which a new generation has grown up without hope, and has adjusted with grace and jauntiness to lives bounded by pessimism.' *Guardian*

Christina Reid was born and bred in Belfast and emigrated to London in 1987. She was playright-in-residence at the Lyric Belfast (1983-4) and at the Young Vic (1988-9). She is currently writing a commissioned play for the Young Vic.

Previous plays which have been produced at home and abroad on stage, television and radio include **The Last of a Dyin' Race** (Winner of the Giles Cooper Award 1986) and **My Name Shall I Tell You My Name**.

Methuen New Theatrescripts series offers frontline intelligence of the most original and exciting work from the fringe.

The Belle of the Belfast City

Did You Hear the One About the Irishman...?

Two Plays by

Christina Reid

methuen

A Methuen New Theatrescript

*First published in Great Britain as an original paperback in 1989 by
Methuen Drama, Michelin House, 81 Fulham Road, London SW3 6RB
and distributed in the United States by HEB Inc., 70 Court Street,
Portsmouth, New Hampshire 03801
Copyright © 1989 by Christina Reid*

British Library Cataloguing in Publication Data

Reid, Christina
The belle of the Belfast city; & Did you hear
the one about the Irishman? – (Methuen
new theatrescripts)
I. Title   II. Reid, Christina. Did you hear
the one about the Irishman?
822'.914
ISBN 0-413-61480-8

Printed in Great Britain by Expression Printers Ltd, London N7 9DP

Caution

*The photograph on the cover is of the author's mother and Tommy the Banjo player,
circa 1938.*

The Belle of the Belfast City

For Susan Hogg

Published to coincide with its première, *The Belle of the Belfast City* opened at the Lyric Players Theatre, Belfast on May 3rd 1989.

Dolly *77, Northern Irish accent*

Vi *57, Dolly's elder daughter. Northern Irish accent*

Rose *36, Dolly's younger daughter. Northern Irish/English accent*

Belle *18, Rose's daughter. Mixed race. English accent*

Janet *36, Dolly's niece. Northern Irish/Scots accent*

Jack *40, Janet's brother. Northern Irish/Scots accent*

Davy *Indeterminate age. Deaf and dumb* ⎞

Tom *Aristocratic English accent* ⎟

Issac *Northern English accent*   ⎬ *

Customs Man *English accent* ⎟

Peter *Janet's husband. Irish accent.* ⎠

The Ballad of William Bloat was written by Raymond Calvert and *Ballad to a Traditional Refrain* by Maurice James Craig. My sincere thanks to both authors and also to Irene Calvert, Agnes Bernelle, the Blackstaff Press and the Linen Hall Library, Belfast.

*These characters can be played by one actor.

Act One

Scene One

Belfast. November 1986

Dolly *(aged 77) sits looking at a photo album. She wears a dressing gown. Her walking stick is propped against a dressing-up box alongside her chair. The room has many framed photographs, old and new. The largest and most dominant image is of the young* **Dolly** *on a concert poster circa 1925 when she topped the bill in the halls as 'The Belle of the Belfast City'.*

Dolly *(sings)*
I'll tell me ma when I go home
The boys won't leave the girls alone
They pulled my hair they stole my comb
Well that's all right till I go home
She is handsome she is pretty
She is the Belle of the Belfast City
She is courtin' One Two Three
Please won't you tell me who is she.

Davy *taps out the rhythm of the song on the spoons,* **Dolly** *listens, and in the distance, as if she is conjuring it, we hear her family singing. It is 1958.* **Dolly**'s *daughters* **Vi** *(aged 29) and* **Rose** *(8), and her niece* **Janet** *(8) come running to her from the past. They dress up with clothes from the box and perform the song.* **Dolly**'s *nephew (***Janet**'s *brother* **Jack**, *aged 12) beats out a drum rhythm with his hands.* **Jack** *does not dress up nor join in the love and laughter that envelopes the girls. During the singing and dancing,* **Dolly** *joins in and becomes an agile woman of 49. Her 18 year old granddaughter* **Belle** *watches with delight.* **Belle** *is in the present time and watches as if seeing an often-heard story recreated.*

Vi, Rose *and* **Janet** *sing.* **Dolly** *joins in.*

Joe Horner says he loves her
All the boys are fightin' for her
They knock at the door and they ring the bell
Saying 'Oh my true love are you well'
Out she comes as white as snow
Rings on her fingers bells on her toes
Oul Dolly Dunbar says she'll die
If she doesn't get the fella with the rovin' eye.

I'll tell me ma when I go home

The boys won't leave the girls alone
They pulled my hair they stole my comb
Well that's all right till I go home
She is handsome she is pretty
She is the Belle of the Belfast City
She is courtin' One Two Three
Please won't you tell me who is she.

Back to the present time. **Jack** *and* **Janet** *exit.* **Dolly** *looks at the photo album.* **Vi** *is in the family shop with* **Davy.** **Belle** *and* **Rose** *are in Aldergrove Airport, Belfast, waiting for transport to the family home.*

Belle She is my grandmother. Dolly Dunbar. Child star of the twenties. Songs, recitations and tap dancing. She won a talent competition when she was ten and was top of the bill before she was thirteen. I'm called after her. Not Dolly, but Belle. That was her stage name and my grandfather Joe never called her anything else.

Rose My mother, the Belle of the Belfast City, happened to be performing in an Orange Hall in Belfast one night when my father Joe Horner was at a Lodge meeting in an upstairs room. They say he heard her singing and walked out of the meeting and into the concert like a man under a spell. And that was it. They eloped a fortnight later, and from then on she gave up the stage and did all her dressing-up and singing and dancing just for him.

Vi Our Rose is nuthin' if not romantic. The truth is that my mother's family were still dressin' her up as if she was thirteen instead of goin' on nineteen, an' trailin' her round draughty oul halls to sing to audiences of twenty or thirty. My father took her away from all that, and waited on her hand and foot for the rest of his life. Still, as they say, it's a poor family can't afford to support one lady.

Dolly An' a poor story that doesn't improve with the tellin'.

Rose When I was very small I used to lie in bed with my big sister Vi and listen to our parents gossiping and giggling like a couple of kids in the room next door. When the bed-springs started to creak, our Vi used to stuff cotton wool in my ears.

Vi Forty one mother was when she had our Rose, and me already over the age of consent. It was the talk of the neighbourhood.

Rose Bad enough to be still doing it at their age, but even worse to be enjoying it so much that she was careless enough to get caught. Our Vi was that mortified she wouldn't go out of the house. My mother and father were over the moon.

Dolly (*looking at the album or pointing to one of the framed photos*) He was as proud as a peacock. My Joe. The cock of the North.

Vi Mother! That'll do!

Dolly She always calls me mother when she's bein' prim an' proper. She must of got that from your side of the family Joe. But you see our Rose? She's like *my* ones. Fulla life an' rarin' to go. She's travelled the world you know, takin' pictures. Imagine that!

Rose *walks to* **Belle.**

Rose No sign of the airport bus yet?

Belle It's been delayed indefinitely. There was a demonstration earlier today near Belfast City centre and some of the roads are still blocked.

Rose What sort of a demonstration?

Belle A loyalist protest against the Anglo-Irish Agreement. The speakers were the Reverend Ian Paisley and your cousin Jack.

Rose Welcome to the land of your forefathers, Belle. Come on, let's see if we can get a taxi.

Dolly (*sings*) Let the wind and the rain and the hail blow high
And the snow come tumblin' from the sky
She's as nice as apple pie
And she'll get her own man by and by
When she gets a man of her own
She won't tell her ma when she comes home
Let them all come as they will
For it's Joe Horner she loves still

Scene Two

Dolly *sits in the room off the family shop. The shop is small and sells crisps, sweets, cigarettes, newspapers, magazines and a few groceries and carry out snacks (sandwiches, pies etc). There is a small table and chairs for the occasional customer to eat on the premises.*

Vi *is setting out the local magazines which have been delivered by* **Davy** *who is deaf and dumb.* **Vi** *and* **Davy** *communicate through hand signals. If* **Vi** *has her back to* **Davy** *he attracts her attention by clapping his hands.*

The shop is in East Belfast in a side street that the Army has closed to traffic.

Jack *walks into the street. He is very neatly and expensively dressed and wears slightly tinted glasses. He moves silently. All* **Jack**'s *movements are very careful and controlled.*

Vi *takes two bars of chocolate from a shelf.*

Vi Thanks for bringin' the magazines round Davy. Here, that's for you and one for your mother. Don't you be eatin' both of them, mind.

Davy *shakes his head and signals thanks.* **Jack** *has come into the shop quietly without* **Vi** *and* **Davy** *being aware of him. He deliberately moves one of the chairs to make a noise.*

Vi God Jack, you made me jump!

Jack They say that's the sign of a bad conscience Vi.

Vi A bad conscience? Me? Huh! Chance would be a fine thing!

Dolly (*sings*) There was an oul woman down Donegall Street, who went to the doctor 'cause she couldn't . . .

Vi Mother!

Jack Aunt Dolly sounds in fine form the day.

Vi Did you ever know a day when she wasn't?

Davy *becomes aware of* **Jack** *and talks rapidly in sign language to* **Vi**. *He is very excited that* **Jack** *is there.*

Vi He says can he get you anything Mr Horner? A cup of tea, a sandwich, a hot pie . . .

Jack Tell him no . . . thanks. I have to go to a meeting. (**Vi** *signals to* **Davy** *who looks crestfallen.*) I just called to ask you if you're still thinking of selling the shop.

Vi (*glancing nervously towards the room where* **Dolly** *sits*) It's not something I've thought out Jack, nor mentioned to nobody else . . . why do you ask?

Jack I have a friend who's looking for a shop and dwelling around here.

Vi What friend?

Jack Nobody you know. A business acquaintance. An Englishman. He's in Belfast for a few days, looking at property. I mentioned this place to him and he's very interested. It's the right size and in the right area. He's got the money to make you a good offer.

Davy *signals to* **Vi** *again.*

Vi Have a quick cup. Just to please him, Jack. The kettle's already boiled, it won't take a minute, and you can have a wee word with Dolly.

She signals to **Davy** *that* **Jack** *will have a cup of tea.* **Davy** *is delighted and almost runs behind the counter.* **Vi** *moves quickly towards the other room, anxious that* **Jack** *won't pursue the subject of selling the shop.* **Jack** *follows her.*

Vi Here's Jack to see you, mother.

Dolly Jack who?

Vi Our Jack.

Dolly The one with the haircut that's never off the television?

Vi You know right well who he is, now stop actin' the eejit.

Dolly *points out a photo to* **Jack**.

Dolly That's you, with a face like a Lurgan spade as usual. An' that's me, and Rose and Vi and your wee sister Janet, God love her. My Joe took that photo the week after we brought the two of you here to live with us. (*Pause.*) Janet's stoppin' here again ye know. Left her man. Don't know what's goin' on there at all. (*At* **Vi**.*) Nobody never tells me nuthin' these days.

Jack *looks sharply at* **Vi**. **Vi** *looks away.* **Dolly** *reaches out as if to take off* **Jack**'s *glasses.* **Jack** *recoils.*

Dolly I only wanted to have a look at your sore eye.

Jack (*off guard*) I haven't got a sore . . . (*He stops, realising that* **Dolly** *is making fun of him.*)

Vi Mother! Behave yourself!

Jack *walks angrily back to the shop.* **Vi** *gives* **Dolly** *an exasperated look.* **Dolly** *smiles innocently.* **Vi** *follows* **Jack**. **Davy** *rushes forward eagerly with a cup of tea for* **Jack** *and sets it on the table.* **Davy** *signals to* **Vi**.

Vi He says, God bless you John Horner, and God bless Ian Paisley. He says you're the boys'll see Ulster right.

Jack What's all this about Janet!

Vi She's left Peter. She's been here about a week.

Jack Why wasn't I told!

Vi She didn't want . . .

Jack You should have phoned me immediately.

Vi It wasn't my place.

Jack What's happened?

Vi I don't know. She won't say.

Jack She'll say to me. Where is she?

Vi She's out.

Jack You tell her I'll be back and I want to see her. Has *he* been here?

Vi Just the once. Peter hasn't a lot of free time. The RUC are on full standby, what with one thing and another . . .

Jack I knew no good would come of that marriage. Sneaking off to a registry office instead of standing up and declaring themselves without shame in the eyes of the Lord. I suppose he's got himself another woman. Catholic licentiousness. It never leaves them.

Vi Peter's a good man.

Jack A Catholic policeman! It's the like of him who've infiltrated the Royal Ulster Constabulary. Corrupted the force into fighting against us instead of standing alongside us as they've always done.

Dolly (*recites loudly*) Holy Mary Mother of God
Pray for me and Tommy Todd
For he's a Fenian and I'm a Prod
Holy Mary mother of God.

Jack That old woman should be in a home!

Vi If that old woman hadn't taken you and Janet in when your mother died, that's where you'd have ended up, in a home! And don't you ever forget that Jack!

Jack I'm sorry if I offended you Vi, I . . .

Vi You offended *her*. This family never bad mouths it's own.

Jack I apologize. I said it without thinking. Not like me. One of the first things you learn in politics. Never speak without knowing exactly what you're going to say . . . I was angry with Janet. That marriage has always been a thorn in my side. (*He becomes aware of* **Davy** *watching them.*) Does he understand what we've been talking about?

Vi No. He needs to be close up and facing you to lip read.

Jack I don't want family business gossiped about.

Vi I don't think you need worry about Davy doin' much gossipin', Jack. (*She signals and talks to* **Davy**.) Away in and sit with Dolly for a while and look at the photos. Here. (*Putting some sweets in a bag.*) Share these with her.

Davy *goes to* **Dolly**. *Holds out the bag of sweets.* **Dolly** *takes one. Turns up her nose and calls to* **Vi**.

Dolly Brandy Balls! Are they not makin' it in bottles anymore? (*She turns the pages in the photo album.* **Davy** *gets excited and points when he sees* **Jack** *as a boy.*) Aye, that's Jack when he was a wee lad, wearin' the national health specs. Suited him better than them Miama Vice jobs he wears these days.

In the shop, **Jack** *stands hesitantly as* **Vi**, *still angry at what he has said, tidies up the magazines.*

Jack You wouldn't fall out with me, would you Vi? We've always been friends, haven't we?

Vi Yes of course we have.

Jack I've always appreciated what your parents did for me and Janet. I'm not ungrateful. But I . . .

Vi It's alright. Jack.

Jack I just want you to know that I've not forgotten how *you* looked after *me* . . . Dolly always sided with Janet and Rose . . . you're the only person in the world I've ever enjoyed singing with . . . do you know that? (*They are both awkward about this declaration.*) Do you still sing?

Vi There's no children here to sing for anymore, and she does enough singin' for both of us.

Jack You had a good voice.

Vi You weren' so bad yourself.

Dolly (*sings*) In the county Tyrone near the town of Dungannon,
Where many's the ruction myself had a hand in
Bob Williamson lived there, a weaver by trade
And all of us thought him a stout Orange blade.

On the Twelfth of July as it yearly did come,
Bob played on the flute to the sound of the drum

You may talk of your harp, your piano or lute
But nothing could sound like the oul Orange flute

Vi (*to* **Jack**) We used to sing it better than that. When you were a wee lad.

(*Sings.*) But Bob the deceiver, he took us all in
And married a Papish called Brigid McGinn
Turned Papish himself and forsook the oul cause
That gave us our freedom, religion and laws.

Jack (*sings*) Now the boys in the townland made comment upon it
And Bob had to flee to the province of Connaught
He flew with his wife and his fixin's to boot
And along with the latter the oul Orange flute

Vi At the chapel on Sundays to atone for past deeds
Bob said Paters and Aves and counted his beads
Til after some time at the priest's own desire
Bob went with his oul flute to play in the choir

Jack And all he could whistle and finger and blow
To play Papish music he found it no go.
'Kick the Pope' and 'Boyne Water' and such like it would sound.
But one Papish squeak in it couldn't be found.

Vi At the council of priests that was held the next day
They decided to banish the oul flute away.
For they couldn't knock heresy out of its head
And they bought Bob another to play in its stead.

Jack So the oul flute was doomed and its fate was pathetic.
It was fastened and burned at the stake as heretic
As the flames licked around it they heard a strange noise
'Twas the oul flute still playin' 'The Protestant Boys!'

Dolly *points to the album and cackles with laughter.* **Jack**'s *rare moment of pleasure is broken.*

Jack And then Rose came sneaking in and took a photo of us.

Vi She meant no harm. I never could understand why you were in such a state about it.

Jack I don't like being caught off guard like that. Rose always was a sly one. (*Hurriedly in case* **Vi** *objects to him slighting one of the family.*) When's she arriving?

Vi Now how did you know about that?

Jack You must have told me.

Vi I haven't seen you since Rose phoned to tell me that her and Belle were coming.

Jack She's bringing her daughter here?

Vi She is indeed. And about time too. That child's over eighteen and been all over the world with our Rose and never in her own home town. It's a disgrace so it is. I told Rose, now that Dolly's not able to travel to London no more you'll have to bring Belle here to see us. She must have took it to heart, for the pair of them are arrivin' the day . . . and would you look at the state of this place. (*She fusses about tidying the shop.*) Don't mind me gettin' on Jack, I don't want Belle thinkin' we run this shop like a midden. I want her to think well of Belfast and have a holiday she'll never forget.

Jack Oh, Rose is on holiday is she?

Vi (*slightly puzzled at his tone of voice*) Aye, and Belle's on half term from her college.

Jack What's she like, this daughter of Rose's?

Vi Like you. Clever. She's studying drama and Irish History at University. I suppose she gets the drama from Dolly. And she's beautiful lookin' too. Mind you it's over a year since I've seen her, but Rose keeps us up to date with photos. Great they are, but then they would be wouldn't they, it's Rose's job. Janet brought some lovely photos back from London. Would you like to see . . .

Jack Nobody told me that Janet had been in London.

Vi You're not around much these days to be told anything, Jack.

Davy *comes back into the shop. He takes a crumpled newspaper cutting out of his pocket. Signals to* **Vi.**

Vi He says would you autograph this for him. It's you and Ian Paisley the day of the last strike on the platform at the City Hall.

Jack (*to* **Davy**) A great day. Were you there?

Vi Yes he was there Jack, and that's something I want to talk to you about. Davy's mother asked me if I would ask you to tell him that he's not to go to the big demonstration next Saturday.

Jack I can't do that.

Vi He's deaf. His sight's poor. He shouldn't be in a crowd like that. It's dangerous. His mother is worried sick about him. He won't heed her, but he'll do anything you say. He worships the ground you walk on.

Jack He has faith in me because of what I believe in. I can't weaken that loyalty by telling him not to go to the rally. Every good Protestant must go.

Vi Look at him Jack. In God's name do you need the like of him on the streets of Belfast in order to win! He has a mental age of ten.

Jack Saturday is the first anniversary of the signing of the accursed Anglo-Irish Agreement. Every loyal man woman and child must take to the streets to show the British Government they will never defeat us. Never! Never! Never!

Vi He can't hear the grand speeches Jack. He goes because the flags and the banners and the crowds excite him. The violence excites him.

Jack There will be no violence. It will be a peaceful protest.

Vi You said that last time and look what happened.

Jack It was not our doing. The police created the violence.

Vi There was a riot Jack. I was there. I saw it.

Jack The Catholics riot. We do not. We are a respectable people.

Davy *points proudly to the newspaper cutting. Signals.*

Vi He says that's him there, in the crowd directly in front of the platform.

Jack He must have been there early to get so near the front. You know it's said that simple people like him are truly the Children of God?

Vi Try tellin' that to his mother.

Jack God works in mysterious ways. Ours not to reason why. Don't you consider it miraculous that he can neither hear nor speak, but he knows instinctively what we're fighting for.

Vi He knows because he lip reads the television and reads the papers. He had partial hearing until he was about ten, and before it left him entirely, his mother taught him to read. That's the miracle her love and faith worked when all them clever doctors said it was impossible. He's all she has Jack. Please tell him not to go.

Jack God will look after him.

Dolly (*sings*) I don't care if it rains or freezes
I am safe in the arms of Jesus.
I am Jesus little lamb.
Yes by Jesus Christ I am.

Jack *takes the newspaper cutting from* **Davy** *and signs it.* **Rose** *and* **Belle**
come into the shop.

Rose Shop!

Vi Oh Rose, you're here! And Belle – look at you all grown up!
You're not a child anymore. You're a young woman. Not too big to
give your oul aunt a hug are you?

A lot of hugging and kissing between the women. **Rose** *becomes aware of*
Jack.

Rose Hello Jack.

Jack Hello Rose, how are you?

Rose I'm very well. And you?

Jack I'm well too, thanks be to God.

Rose This is my daughter Belle. Belle, this is my cousin John
Horner. Jack to the family.

Belle Hello Jack.

She half moves to shake his hand but doesn't as he just nods his head
slightly to acknowledge the introduction.

Vi And this is Davy McBride, lives round the corner, gives me a
hand in the shop nigh an' again.

Belle Hello Davy.

She holds out her hand to **Davy** *who has been staring at her since she came*
in. He hesitantly touches her hand then shyly almost touches her face. Stops
and signals to **Vi**.

Vi (*laughs*) He's all of a dither because he's never seen nobody with
dark skin before, except on the television.

Belle Is this a joke?

Rose There aren't many like you in Belfast Belle. And those that
are, are well-to-do. Restaurant owners, doctors, university lecturers,
overseas students. They don't live round here.

Belle No working-class black ghettos?

Rose None.

Belle (*looking directly at* **Jack**) No prejudice?

Davy *signals to* **Vi** *again.*

Vi *shakes her head at him and looks sideways at* **Belle** *who grins, and surprises* **Vi** *by signalling to* **Davy** *as she talks.*

Belle No Davy, I'm not from Africa. I'm from England. And my mother is from Belfast and my father is from America. I think that makes me an Anglo/Irish Yank.

Vi Now where did you learn to do that?

Belle I have a friend who's deaf.

Vi Isn't that great. Now Davy'll have three people to talk to. You me an' his mother. It was *her* taught *me*. (*She looks at* **Jack**.) She's a nice wee woman.

Davy *signals self-consciously to* **Belle**.

Belle Thank you Davy. I may take you up on that.

He signals goodbye to everyone, then shakes **Belle**'*s hand and leaves very quickly. He passes* **Janet** *in the street and signals to her excitedly and runs off.* **Janet** *stands for a moment outside.*

Rose What did he say?

Belle He offered to be my escort if I want to see Belfast.

Vi Hey girl, I think you've clicked there.

Jack I must go.

Rose Affairs of state Jack?

Jack Think over what I mentioned Vi. And don't forget to tell Janet I want to talk to her. (**Rose** *and* **Vi** *exchange looks.*) I see *you* know about it.

Rose I know she's here. She phoned me.

Jack She tells everybody but not her own brother.

Rose Some things are easier discussed between women.

Jack Women! That's always been the trouble with this house. Women having secrets, whispering, gossiping.

VI I told you Jack, I don't know anything to gossip about.

Jack But *you* do. Don't you, Rose.

Janet *comes in. There is a strained silence.*

Jack I'm late for a meeting. I'll talk to you later, madam.

He walks out.

Belle God, he's a bundle of laughs isn't he?

VI He's under a lot of strain at the moment. He's alright when you get to know him. (**Rose** *and* **Janet** *exchange looks.*) And we'll have less of the looks between you two if you don't mind. It's a long time since this family were all together under one roof, and I want it to be happy. Like the old days. No troubles.

Janet I'm sorry. This is all my fault.
Rose (*sharply*) No it's not Janet! (*More gently.*) You have got to stop always blaming yourself when it's Jack who's at fault.
Dolly (*sings*) In and out go the dusty bluebells
In and out go the dusty bluebells
In and out go the dusty bluebells
I'll be your master.
Tapper-rapper-rapper on her left hand shoulder
Tapper-rapper-rapper on her left hand shoulder
Tapper-rapper-rapper on her left hand shoulder
I'll be your master.

Scene Three

Dolly *and* **Belle** *sit turning the pages in the photo album.*

Belle Not so fast. I want you to tell me about every one of them. What age everybody is. Where you were at the time. What you were doing. I want to know all about my family. I want to know all about Ireland.

Dolly Well, I can tell you all about the family. But as for Ireland. I've lived here all my life and I still can't make head nor tail of it. Better leave that to them clever professors at your university.

Belle So many photographs.

Dolly Aye, my Joe was a dab hand with a camera. That was one of the last photos he ever took, God rest him. That's me and your mammy and Janet and Vi settin' off one August mornin' for the

Dublin train. I give your mammy Joe's oul camera after he died, an' she took to it like a duck in water. Then me an' Vi bought her a good camera when she was older an' she's never looked back since.

Belle You all look so happy.

Dolly We had good times. Outin's an' parties an' sing songs an' dressin' up, you don't know the half of it.

Belle It must be lovely being part of a big family.

Dolly You *are* part of a big family.

Belle I mean, having a big family around you all the time. A granny who lives nearby. I miss you not coming to London.

Dolly I've missed you too. You'll have to come here now and see me. I'm sure Rose misses you now you're at the university.

Belle She's alright. She has lots of friends.

Dolly Friends are not the same as family. Does she have a man?

Belle Sort of.

Dolly Oh aye. Does that mean he's married?

Belle No. It means that *he* has *his* flat and *she* has *hers*. She's an independent woman, my mother.

Dolly She always was. She takes that after me.

Belle But you ran off and got married before you were nineteen.

Dolly But I was never a housewife. My Joe never wanted that. He was a rare bird. An Ulsterman who could cook.

Pause.

Belle Did you ever meet *my* father?

Dolly Not at all. We knew nothin' about any of it till you were born an' he was back in America by then.

Belle I met him last Christmas, when mum and I were in New York. I told her I wanted to see him and she got in touch with him through some mutual friends. He arranged to meet us in a very expensive restaurant. Bought us lunch. Kept looking over his shoulder in case someone he knew might see us. He's a very respectable married man now. A pillar of a Baptist Church. He made a great point of telling me that he hadn't left my mother. I already knew all that. Rose has never lied to me about anything. I told him that now that I'd met him I could understand why she'd thrown him out. He's a sanctimonious American bible-belt prig. I bet he votes for Ronald Reagan. I asked him what he told his God about me, and he got up and walked away.

Dolly I'm sorry, child.

Belle I'm not. Now that I know what he's like, I can get on with my life knowing I haven't missed much. I didn't like him. I don't like your nephew Jack either. Does he always talk to Janet like that?

Dolly Has that skittery ghost been gettin' at Janet again? I should never have told him that she was here. I only said it to annoy him. To let him know that when Janet was in trouble it was us she come to an' not him.

Belle Why is she afraid of him?

Dolly I thought I'd put a stop to all that years ago. But maybe it was too deep ingrained by the time me and Joe got them. God knows what went on before that. Their father was a Presbyterian Minister you know. Joe's only brother, Martin. Martin died young an' the mother took the two childer back to Scotland where she come from. An oul targe of a schoolteacher she was. You know the sort. Goes to church on Sunday, an' prays to God to give her strength to beat the kids on Monday.

Belle She beat them?

Dolly Into the ground. Not with a big stick. With words. Words like, sin, the world and the devil. And the worst sins were the sinful lusts of the flesh. Jack's job as the man of the house, was to protect his sister from temptation. I used to wonder how his mother and Martin ever had kids. I mean it's not as if they were Catholic an' he could dip it in the Holy Water first. May God forgive her an' Jack for the way they scared that wee girl, for I know I never will. Do you know, the day me an' Joe arrived in Scotland to get them, I picked Janet up an' she stiffened like a ramrod. An' then she sort of crumpled up an' she cried, an' she fell asleep in my arms. Eight years old an' nobody had ever cuddled her. That's what I call a sin.

Belle And what about Jack?

Dolly Jack doesn't like bein' touched. Did ye not notice? I suppose that's why he never married.

Belle I thought perhaps it was just me he didn't want to touch.

Dolly Do ye come in for much of that? I mean, is it a bother to ye, bein' neither one thing nor the other?

Belle Only when it bothers other people.

Dolly Well, you needn't worry about round here, love. All they're interested in is what religion ye are.

Belle Do you believe in God, gran?

Dolly I believe I'll be with my Joe someday, an' I hope it'll be soon.

Belle Oh no, gran!

Dolly Ach, I don't mean right this minute love. I'm all right for the time being'. But I don't want to outlive my time. End up bein' kep' goin' by machines in a hospital. I have a horror of that. I can cope with not bein' able to dance with my feet no more. But I couldn't cope with not bein' able to dance in my head. I want to go under my own steam when my time comes. If you're around, will you see to that?

Very slight pause.

Belle Yes, I will.

Dolly I knew you'd say that, without a moral debate. You think straight. You see clear. Like me. Vi's too responsible, an' Rose is too romantic, an' Janet . . . . Janet's fallin' to bits an' I think I know why, but I can't say till I know for sure. The rest of them think I'm a daft oul woman who can't be told certain things. But I know more about life than they'll ever know. It's got nuthin' to do with age. I was born knowin'. Like you. (*Pause.*) Will you tell me what happened to Janet in London?

Belle Yes, I will.

*She takes **Dolly**'s hands and talks quietly to her about **Janet**. In the shop **Rose** is helping **Vi** to clean and tidy.*

Vi Man that's great. It's weeks since I had the time to give the place a proper reddin' out.

Rose Do you do much business, Vi?

Vi Not the way we used to. Since the army closed the street to traffic, we don't get the passin' trade. An' apart from that we can't compete with the prices in the new supermarket. I've cut out most of the groceries. But we get by on the snacks, an' people comin' in for the cigarettes an' the papers an' the magazines.

Rose *has been looking at some of the magazines as she tidies the rack.*

Rose Why do you sell thus stuff Vi?

Vi It's what all the shops round here sell. It's a good local paper for local people.

Rose (*holding out a copy of 'Ulster'*) And what about this load of racist propaganda?

Vi What are ye talkin' about? The U.D.A. aren't against the blacks.

Rose Racism is not necessarily to do with colour, Vi.

Vi Don't you be startin' on one of your grand political speeches, Rose. You're only back five minutes. Give your tongue a rest. An' put that magazine back in its place. An' don't be creasin' them, or they won't sell, an' I'll have to pay for them.

Rose What else do you have to pay them for, Vi?

Vi What do you mean?

Rose I mean the man in the black leather jacket, who came in late last night for a sandwich. Does everybody who buys a sandwich here get a sealed envelope with it?

Vi We've always given to the Loyalist Prisoners Fund.

Rose That was no voluntary contribution in a collecting tin. That was notes by prior arrangement. How much do they make you pay, Vi?

Vi They protect the shop.

Rose From what?

Vi From vandals.

Rose You give them money and in return, they tell their vandals not to break your windows. Is that it? Or are you afraid they'll publish your name in their 'Did you Know' column? (*She reads from the 'Ulster Magazine'.*) Did you know that Paul Reilly & Sons, building contractors in Newry, employ workmen from the Irish Republic. Are these I.R.A. spies working in your area? . . . Did you know that the new canteen manageress in the Protestant owned firm of Spencer Brothers is a Catholic and has a brother with known terrorist links in the town. Staff and customers who have any links with the security forces – Beware! Do you never worry Vi, that you might sell this distorted information to a customer who'll go out of this shop and shoot an innocent canteen manageress!

Vi Don't you lecture me, Rose! It's all very fine and easy living' in London and makin' noble decisions about what's right and what's wrong about how we live here. I'm the one who has to live here. You've been on your travels since you were seventeen. You don't even talk like us any more. Talk's cheap. And it's easy to be brave when you've somewhere safe to run.

Rose So you admit that you pay them because you're afraid.

Vi I admit nothin'! (*Slight pause.*) I talked to the police about it. They said there was nothin' they could do. Advised me to pay. The sergeant said 'Think of it as doin' your bit to keep the peace Miss Horner. It's cheap at the price.'

Rose What's the going rate for intimidation? Do they give you a discount because John Horner was raised in this house?

Vi Jack has no connection with them. He's a politician.

Rose Jack's a gangster. He's well connected with the Protestant Paramilitaries here, and the other right-wing organizations in the United Kingdom.

Vi Why are you here Rose? It's not just a holiday is it? Jack knew you were comin' before I told him.

Rose Did he now? That's interesting. But not surprising. Jack's English allies are very well informed.

Vi About what?

Janet *comes into the shop from the street.*

Janet Look what I've got. Dulse and yellowman for Belle. (*Pause.*) What's the matter?

Rose Nothing that dulse and yellowman won't cure. Come on. Let's introduce my daughter to the gastronomic delights of her homeland (*They go to* **Dolly** *and* **Belle** .) Hey Belle, Janet's bought you a present.

Belle (*peering into the two small paper bags*) What is it?

Janet The sticky stuff is called yellowman. It's a sort of toffee.

Belle And the black stuff?

Janet It's called dulse. You'll love it. Try a bit.

Belle *eats some dulse. Splutters and coughs.*

Belle What is it?

Janet Dried seaweed.

Belle Dried seaweed!

Rose It's very good for you.

Vi Puts hairs on your chest.

Belle It's revolting!

Dolly It's an acquired taste love. You have to start on it young. This lot were weaned on it.

Vi Have a bit of the yellowman. It'll take the taste of the salt out of your mouth.

Dolly Remember that wee shop in Dublin sold the great yellowman? We always bought some for the train journey home. Look, there's a photo of us all in the station. Laden with pruck.

Belle Pruck?

Vi Pruck. Pickin's. Smuggled goods. Did your mother never tell you that you come from a long line of customs dodgers?

Sound of a train. A British customs officer walks on. **Belle** *watches as* **Dolly**, **Vi Rose** *and* **Janet** *dress up from the box. They assume position as if on a train. They eat the Dulse and Yellowman. The year is 1959.* (**Dolly** *is 50;* **Vi** *30;* **Rose** *9;* **Janet** *9.*)

Dolly (*sings*) At the Oul Lammas Fair boys
Were you ever there.
Were you ever at the fair at Ballycastleo
Did you treat your Mary Ann
To some dulse and yellowman
At the oul Lammas Fair at Ballycastleo

Customs Man Anything to declare ladies?

Dolly Ach no son. Sure me and the wee childer have just been visitin' a sick oul aunt in Dublin. All I've got's the wee drop of whiskey she give me for my man an' a few sweets for the wains. We're allowed that without payin' the duty, aren't we?

Customs Man (*to* **Rose** *and* **Janet**) And did your poor old aunt put the sweets in those pretty little handbags?

They open the bags which contain only sweets.

Dolly (*aside to* **Vi**) The oul get. Searchin' innocent childer. (*She smiles sweetly at the* **Customs Man** *as he turns to her and* **Vi**.)

Customs Man And now you two.

They hold out their bags. He looks inside. Removes a half bottle of whiskey from **Dolly**'s *bag.*

Dolly Like I said son. Just the half bottle.

Customs Man What about your pockets? (*They turn out their pocket linings. They are empty.*) Are you telling me that you've been to the south and haven't bought anything?

Dolly No money son. It was as much as we could do to scrape up the spondulics for the train fares. The oul aunt wanted to see the wains before God took her.

The **Customs Man** *looks totally unconvinced.*

Rose (*quickly, to distract him*) Janet bought an ornament for our bedroom. Show him Janet.

Janet *takes the 'ornament' out of her pocket. It is a religious statue of the Virgin Mary.*

VI Mother of God!
Dolly (*aside to* **Vi**) She didn't know what it was, an' I hadn't the heart to tell her she couldn't have it, she was that taken by it.

VI Jack'll go mad.

Dolly Ach he'll never see it in the girls' bedroom.

Janet It's a pretty lady. Isn't she lovely?

The **Customs Man** *is completely distracted from his suspicions by* **Janet**'s *sweet innocent face. He smiles at her.*

Customs Man It's very nice dear. Have a pleasant journey.

He exits. **Dolly** *laughs delightedly.*

Dolly God. You're great Rose, distractin' him like that. For a minute I thought he was considerin' takin' us off the train for a body search. They took my cousin Annie off the train one time. Made her take all her clothes off. Every stitch. Mortified she was. Particularly when they found the two bottles of whiskey an' the hundred John Players she'd hid in her knickers.

VI Mother!

Janet *and* **Rose** *go to get up*

Dolly Sit down the pair of ye! Yer not to move one inch til we're well clear of the border. Sometimes the oul buggers start the train an' stop it again just to catch ye on.

(*The train noise starts up again. They all sit very still for a minute.*) Right! All clear!

Janet *and* **Rose** *jump to their feet and hand* **Vi** *the smuggled goods they've been sitting on.*

Rose Two bags of sugar, and a carton of cigarettes for daddy.

Janet Two bags of tea and a bottle of gin for auntie Dolly.

Vi *gets up.*

VI Pair of shoes for me an' two bottles of whiskey for my father.

Dolly Never mind all that. Will yous get this curtain material off me before I suffocate!

She gets to her feet and removes her dressing gown. There are layers and layers of lace curtain material wrapped round her body. **Rose** *and* **Janet** *unwind the material by dancing round* **Dolly** *as if she's a Maypole.* **Dolly** *dances and sings.*

Dolly Our Queen can birl her leg
Birl her leg, birl her leg
Our Queen can birl her leg
Birl her leg leg leg.
All (*sing*) Our Queen can ate a hard bap
Ate a hard bap, ate a hard bap
Our Queen can ate a hard bap
Ate a hard bap bap bap

Dolly *puts her dressing gown on again and falls exhausted back into her seat.*

Dolly Now I know how a swaddled child feels. I thought I was gonna expire with the heat. Oh dear God I forgot about the sausages. They must be half cooked in the perspiration.

She removes a package from her brassiere.

Rose What's that mammy?

Dolly Two poun' of Haffners sausages. Best sausages in Ireland. They're for Jack's Church Brigade Supper the marra night.

Rose Jack won't eat anything that was made in the South of Ireland.

Dolly Jack won't know where they come from. Nor how they were smuggled over the border. With any luck they'll choke the Church Lad's Brigade.

Rose Can we tell Jack after they've eaten them, mammy?

Dolly I don't see why not, darlin'

VI You're a wicked woman mother, an' stop encouragin' them wee ones to be the same.

Dolly Our Rose doesn't need any encouragin', do ye love?

The group freezes with the exception of **Janet** *who lifts the statue and dances into the shop. She sings quietly.*

Janet Our Queen can birl her leg
Birl her leg birl her leg
Our Queen . . .

She stops singing as **Jack** *as a boy of thirteen walks towards her.*

Jack What's that you've got?

Janet She's my pretty lady. I bought her in Dublin.

Jack *grabs the statue. Shouts at* **Janet** .

Jack That's no pretty lady. It's a blasphemous Popish statue. A heathen image of Christ's mother. Thou shalt not make unto thee any graven image, or any likeness of any thing that is in heaven above, or that is in the earth beneath, or that is in the water under the earth. Thou shalt not bow down thyself to them, nor serve them; for I the Lord thy God am a jealous God, visiting the iniquity of the fathers upon the children unto the third and fourth generation of them that hate me. You have sinned Janet. You have broken the fourth commandment. You must be punished.

Janet Leave me alone. I'll tell aunt Dolly.

Jack No you won't, or God will punish you. You must repent, you must atone. You have broken His commandment. Now you must break this.

He holds out the statue.

Janet No!

Jack Then I must break it for you. I am the guardian of your faith.

He raises the statue above his head.

Janet If you hurt her I'll tell the Church Brigade about the sausages!

Jack What?

Janet Nothing.

Jack What did you say! What about the sausages?

Janet Nothing.

Jack *grabs her. Twists her arm.*

Jack Tell me! Tell me!

Janet They were from Dublin. Dolly bought them. It wasn't me!

Jack Women! Women! Temptation! Deception! You're the instruments of the devil! The root of all evil!

He smashes the statue on the shop counter and scatters the pieces. Turns furiously towards **Janet***.*

Janet Leave me alone! Leave me alone!

Jack *exits.* **Janet** *continues shouting. The frozen group look up. It is 1986 again.*

Dolly In the name of God, what was that! Where's Janet?

Rose I'll go.

Vi *moves to follow* **Rose** *into the shop.*

Dolly No Vi. Sit down. I want to talk to you about Janet. (*To* **Belle**.) She has to be told, Belle. This family always looks after its own, no matter what. And maybe it's Vi's common sense that's needed here as much as anything else.

Rose *finds* **Janet** *kneeling on the floor in the shop, sobbing and picking up little pieces of the broken statue.*

Janet Shattered . . . Shattered . . . Not just seven . . . twenty seven . . . twenty seven years bad luck . . . the luck of the Irish . . . the luck of the devil. . . .

Rose Janet.

Janet Too many little pieces. It can never be put right.

Rose *picks up a piece of broken china.*

Rose It's only a plate. One of the cheap ones Vi uses in the shop.

Janet Cheap . . . damaged goods . . . like me . . .

Rose No.

Janet Every morning I waken filled with the knowledge of him.
And I think maybe I dreamt it. Maybe I made it up. But I didn't.
And I don't know what to do. Tell me what to do, Rose.

Rose I don't know what you want.

Janet I want it never to have happened.

Rose Why?

Janet Sin.

Rose No. Sex.

Janet And shame.

Rose What are you ashamed of?

Janet I don't feel quilty, and I should feel guilty. I need to feel
guilty.

Rose Why?

Janet There is no forgiveness without repentance.
And I'm not sorry.

Rose Good.

Janet Good? I go to a party in London. I spend all that night and
most of the next day in bed with a . . . a boy . . .

Rose Martin should be so flattered. He's twenty six if he's a day.

Janet And I am thirty six and married.

Rose To Peter Pan. You can't be worried about *him* forgiving you.
He forgives everybody.

Janet I never give Peter a thought. All I think about is Martin. His
face, his hair, his hands, his smell. Maybe I'm possessed. Maybe
Martin is the devil my mother said was always there. Waiting at your
shoulder. Fornication. Adultery. Adultery. Adultery . . .

Rose Stop it! Stop it! That's Jack talking. Not you.

Janet Ashes to ashes. Dust to dust.
If the Lord don't get you, the devil must.
Jack won't rest till he knows.

Rose There's no need for Jack to know.

Janet He'll make me tell him.

Rose You don't have to tell Jack anything. It's none of his business. He's only your brother. Not your keeper. Not your God. You don't need Jack's permission to do anything. You're a grown woman.

Janet I've been avoiding Vi. Can't look her straight in the face. What am I going to tell her?

Rose Whatever you want to tell her.

Janet I want to tell her the truth. She'll despise me.

Rose Don't be daft. She'll be a bit shocked, and then she'll get over it, and then she'll be on your side regardless of what she thinks, because you're family and the family always comes first with Vi. You know that.
Remember when Belle was born? Vi was on the next plane to London. I didn't ask her to do that. She just came. Before they brought Belle in from the nursery. I said to her, 'Vi, so that it doesn't come as a bit of a shock, I think you should know that although the father's Protestant, he's not exactly what you'd call a white Anglo-Saxon.' And Vi just gave me one of her long looks and she said, 'See you Rose? If there's an awkward way of doin' a thing, you'll find it.'

The telling of this story has relaxed **Janet**. *She manages a smile.*

Janet Does Martin care about me at all?

Rose (*carefully*) Martin, like Peter, fell in love with your innocence.

Janet And now that's gone. And so has Martin.

Rose He's married.

Janet I know. He told me. Before we went to bed. So I can't even claim I was tricked. Or seduced. I don't even feel guilty about that. It wasn't true when I said I wish it had never happened. It was everything I ever dreamt it might be. Did you love Belle's father like that?

Rose I suppose I did. At first. Don't remember it clearly anymore. It's a romantic notion that first love is always an unforgettable special, never-to-be-equalled experience. I've had better love since. What I remember most clearly about Belle's father is how inadequate and dependent he made me feel. How outraged he was when I turned down his noble offer to make an honest women of me. Admitting that it was a fucking shambles made an honest woman of me.

Janet Peter wants me to come home. I had a letter from him this morning.

Rose What do you want?

Janet Remember the little girl in the Just William stories who wanted to scream and scream and scream? (*She walks away from* **Rose.** *Talks to herself as if in a dream.*) I want what I can't have. I want it to be like it was. Like the old days in the photo album. I want Dolly to put her arms around me and sing me to sleep. And when I waken, I want Jack to have gone away for ever. And Peter too. I'm tired being the sister of a devil and the wife of a saint.

Jack *walks on stage.*

Peter *in R.U.C. uniform walks on from the other side.*

Janet *is situated centre stage between them. She looks from one to the other.*

Peter Green gravel, Green gravel
Your grass is so green
You're the fairest young damsel
That ever I've seen
Green gravel, Green gravel
Your true lover's dead.
So I've sent you a letter
To turn round your head
I washed her and I dressed her
And I robed her in silk
And I wrote down her name
With a glass pen and ink.
Green Gravel, Green Gravel
Your grass is so green
You're the fairest young damsel
That ever I've seen.

Jack (*quoting from St Paul*) It is good for a man not to marry. But since there is so much immorality each man should have his own wife and each woman her own husband. The husband should fulfil his marital duty to his wife, and likewise the wife to her husband. The wife's body does not belong to her alone, but also to the husband. In the same way, the husband's body does not belong to him alone but also to his wife. Do not deprive each other except by mutual consent. Then come together again so that Satan will not tempt you because of your lack of self control. I say this as a concession, not as a command. I wish that all men were as I am.

Peter I love you. Come back to me.

Jack I love you. Come back to me.

Janet Out of the frying pan into the fire. A devil and a saint are the same thing. Afraid of women. Afraid we'll tempt you. Afraid we won't. They say there are no women in Ireland. Only mothers and sisters and wives. I'm a sister and a wife. But I'll never be a mother. Will I Peter? Why did you marry me? Why did I marry you? (*To* **Jack**.) Because he was everything you were not. Quiet. Gentle. Kind. After the ceremony we went to Dublin for a week. It was the one city I could be sure you wouldn't be in. But you were with me, all the way there on the train. (*To* **Peter**.) It was very late when we got to the hotel. I wanted you to take me . . . to teach me . . . I wanted to exorcize him . . . to find out that it wasn't an act of sin and shame and pain and guilt. But as soon as you touched me I turned away. And then I turned back to you and you said. 'It's been a long day. Let's go to sleep.' The next day we hired a car and drove around Dublin. When we got back to the hotel we were both very tired. You told me that there was nothing to worry about. You said lots of newly married couples didn't . . . for a while. You said there was no hurry. I felt grateful because you were so patient, so kind. It was years before I realized that you were relieved, that you didn't want . . . had never wanted . . . that you were content with things that way.

(*To* **Jack**.) And I suppose I was content too. Knowing that I would never have to contend with you and Peter's mother fighting over the religion of the children of this unholy union. Peter's very fond of children. He's a community policeman. Does a lot of work with teenagers. One of them asked him once. 'Why does an Irish Catholic join a sectarian force like the Royal Ulster Constabulary?' And Peter said, 'It will always be a sectarian force if Catholics never join.' He was such a good little boy that his mother expected him to become a priest, but Peter sees his mission in life as doing something more positive towards peace and reconciliation.

(*To* **Peter**.) Was marrying me part of that mission?

Peter I love you.

Janet I am not your mother! I am not your sister!

Jack I love you.

Janet I am not your virgin mother, nor your virgin wife!

Peter I love you. Come back to me.

Jack I love you. Come back to me.

Janet *throws back her head and screams.* **Rose** *runs to her. The two men exit.* **Janet** *runs past* **Rose** *to* **Dolly**. **Vi** *storms into the shop and shouts at* **Rose**.

Vi What have you and your loose-livin' English friends done to that child! Look at the state of her!

Rose She's not a child!

Vi (*indicating to where* **Dolly** *and* **Belle** *are comforting* **Janet**) You call that bein' grown-up.

Rose It's a damn sight more grown up than living in Never Never Land!

Vi By God you have a lot to answer for.

Rose When in doubt always find a woman to blame. If it's answers you want, ask Peter, ask Jack!

Vi And what about this Martin. This so-called friend of yours! I suppose he has nuthin' to answer for either! A married man in no position to stand by her. The road to nowhere. And you set her on it. May God forgive you.

Dolly *sits cradling* **Janet**'s *head in her lap. She strokes* **Janet**'s *hair and sings.*

Dolly I know where I'm goin'
And I know who's goin' with me
I know who I love
But the dear knows who I'll marry.

I'll wear gowns of silk
And shoes of fine green leather
Ribbons for my hair
And a ring for every finger.

I know who is sick
And I know who is sorry
I know who I've kissed
But God knows who I'll marry.

Some says he's black
But I say he's bonny
The darlin' of my heart
My handsome winsome Johnnie.

Act Two

Janet *sits at* **Dolly***'s feet, looking through the photo album.* **Belle** *walks on and watches* **Dolly** *and* **Janet** *from the other side of the stage.* **Dolly** *recites.*

Dolly In a mean abode on the Shankill Road
Lived a man called William Bloat
He had a wife, the curse of his life,
Who continually got his goat.
So one day at dawn, with her nightdress on,
He cut her bloody throat.

With a razor gash he settled her hash,
Oh never was crime so quick,
But the steady drip on the pillow slip
Of her lifeblood made him sick,
And the pool of gore on the bedroom floor
Grew clotted cold and thick.

And yet he was glad that he'd done what he had.
When she lay there stiff and still,
But a sudden awe of the angry law
Struck his soul with an icy chill.
So to finish the fun so well begun,
He resolved himself to kill.

Then he took the sheet off his wife's cold feet,
And twisted it into a rope.
And he hanged himself from the pantry shelf.
'Twas an easy end, let's hope.
In the face of death with his latest breath,
He solemnly cursed the Pope.

But the strangest turn to the whole concern
Is only just beginnin'
He went to Hell but his wife got well,
And she's still alive and sinnin'
For the razor blade was German made,
But the sheet was Irish linen.

Belle Before I came here, I had two images of Belfast. A magical one conjured by my grandmother's songs and stories and recitations, and a disturbing one of the marches and banners and bands on the six o'clock news . . . They are both true, but not the whole truth of this bizarre and beautiful city. Belfast is surrounded by soft green hills. All its inhabitants live within walking distance of the countryside, and like village people they are inquisitive, friendly, hospitable.

Belfast must be the best kept social secret in the British Isles . . . There was a bomb scare in Marks and Spencers today. A voice from a loud speaker asked the customers to evacuate the building. Nobody panicked. Nobody ran. The general feeling was one of annoyance that the shopping had been interrupted. One woman was very cross because the girl at the checkout wouldn't finish ringing through her purchases. 'It'll be another one of them hoax calls,' she said. And it was.

I wasn't frightened by the bomb scare, but I was frightened by their complacency, by their irritated acceptance that it's a normal part of everyday life, like being searched before entering the shops. The situation has existed for so long now that the people have come to accept the abnormal as normal. Armed soldiers in suburban streets. Armed police in armoured cars. An acceptable level of violence. There's a new generation of citizens who've never known it to be any other way.

I accepted Davy's offer to show me around but discovered that he has only ever been round here and the city centre. That's not peculiar to him. Belfast is not so much a city as a group of villages forming an uneasy alliance. My Aunt Vi has lived here all her life and has never set foot in West Belfast. Injun Country. The Badlands. Her images of the Falls Road are conjured by Nationalist songs and stories and recitations. And the news bulletins and the rhetoric of the Reverend Ian Paisley confirm everything she fears to be true. She votes for the Unionist Party to keep the Republican Party out.

Dolly (*sings*) Will you come to our wee party will you come?
Bring your own bread and butter and a bun
You can bring a cup of tea
You can come along with me
Will you come to our wee party will you come?

Will you come to Abyssinia will you come?
Bring your own ammunition and a gun
Mussolini will be there firing bullets in the air
Will you come to Abyssinia will you come?

Belle *walks into the shop where* **Vi** *and* **Rose** *are making sandwiches, and heating sausage rolls.*

Belle I've got party poppers and paper hats.

Vi What's a party popper when it's at home?

Belle It's a sort of friendly hand grenade.

She pulls one of the poppers and covers **Vi** *with streamers.*

Vi Sometimes I wonder if we're all mad or mental in this family.

Belle Why?

Vi Havin' a party in the middle of all these terrible goin's on with Janet.

Belle Janet's looking forward to it.

Rose Mum always has a party on dad's birthday.

Vi Dolly has had a party every day of her life.

Belle I think it's a wonderful idea. What good does it do him or any of us making a mournful pilgrimage to a graveside on a cold November day. Much better to be here, reminiscing and singing and celebrating his life.

Vi It's well seein' who you take after. I tell ye, Dolly'll never be dead as long as you're alive. Come the three minute warnin' an' no doubt the pair of ye'll be organizin' a wee sing-song to pass the time till the bomb goes off. I hope you have your party piece ready. Everybody has to do a turn you know.

Rose Except Jack. Jack only ever did a party piece once because Dolly made him, and he refused ever to do one again.

Belle Jack's been invited?

Vi Of course he has. He's one of the family, whether your mother likes it or not.

Rose He'll only be calling briefly. He has a prior engagement.

Belle Does Janet know he's coming?

Vi She has to face him sooner or later. And I told her, better sooner while the family's all here gathered round her. And I've told Jack he's not to be gettin' at her. She has to work things out for herself.

Rose You didn't tell him about . . .

Vi I did not. And I don't intend to. Least said soonest mended. He'd never understand it. *I* don't understand it. I always thought her and

Peter were the happiest couple in the land. Never a cross word between them, and neither of them lookin' a day older than the day they were wed. And as for this man in London . . .

Belle Sexy Martin? What a way to lose your virginity after fifteen years of celibate marriage. (*She grins at* **Vi** *'s outraged expression.*) Aren't you glad she enjoyed it? Wouldn't it have been awful if she hadn't, after waiting all that time?

Vi I have never heard such talk from a youngster in all my life. When I was your age . . .

Belle I'm the age now that my mother was when she had me.

Vi Maybe my trouble is, I never was that age. I never remember a time when I was really young, the way children are. As soon as I was tall enough to see over the counter, Dolly kept me off school to work in the shop. I tell you, Davy can read and write better than I can.

Dolly (*sings*) Our wee school's a good wee school
It's made of bricks and mortar
And all that's wrong with our wee school's
The baldy headed master
He doesn't care he pulls our hair
He goes to church on Sunday
And prays to God to give him strength
To beat the kids on Monday.

Janet (*as a child*) Auntie Dolly?

Dolly What darlin'?

Janet Can I stay off school tomorrow and help in the shop?

Dolly Now you know what Vi's like about you wee ones missin' your schoolin' unless you're really sick. Not that she was ever all that keen on goin' to school when she was your age. Any excuse to get stayin' at home.

Janet *coughs exaggeratedly.*

Dolly An' there's no point in tryin' it on. It might work with me but it'll never fool Vi.

Vi *and* **Rose** *as a child come in with plates of sandwiches and sausage rolls.* **Jack** *as a boy stands sulking in the street.*

Dolly Where's the Prophet Isaiah?

Rose He's out in the street sulkin'.

Janet He says we should be thanking God for taking Uncle Joe to heaven and not having a sinful party.

Dolly Oh does he indeed. I'll decide how we mourn my Joe. And Jack'll do as he's bid as long as he lives in Joe's house. Vi! Away an' tell him to come in this minute and join the party.

Vi Ach, leave him alone mother.

Rose I'll tell him.

She runs gleefully to the street to fetch **Jack.**

Vi He doesn't like parties.

Dolly He'll sing for Joe along with the rest of the family.

Rose *returns, followed very reluctantly by* **Jack.**

Dolly Right. Now that we're all assembled, how's about 'Soldier, Soldier'. My Joe loved 'Soldier, Soldier'. You can play the man, Jack.

Jack I don't know the words.

Dolly 'Course you do. You've watched the girls often enough.

Jack I don't.

Rose I'll help you.

She smiles sweetly at him. **Jack** *gives her a murderous look.*

Dolly We'll all help you. Where's the dressin' up box, Vi?

Vi It's here.

Dolly Right. Away ye go, Janet. You be the girl.

Belle *watches the performance of the song with the photo album on her knee.* **Janet** *sings the girl's part and fetches the clothes for the soldier from the box.* **Jack**, *assisted by* **Rose**, *sullenly sings the man's part.* **Dolly** *puts the clothes on him when he looks as if he is about to refuse.* **Dolly** *and* **Vi** *and* **Rose** *sing the chorus.* **Jack** *becomes increasingly angry and humiliated as the song progresses.*

Janet Oh soldier, soldier, won't you marry me?
With your musket, fife and drum.

Jack Oh no sweet maid I cannot marry you
For I have no coat to put on

Chorus So, off she went to her grandfather's tent
And got him a coat of the very very best

She got him a coat of the very very best
And the soldier put it on.

Janet Oh soldier, soldier, won't you marry me?
With your musket, fife and drum.

Jack Oh no sweet maid I cannot marry you
For I have no boots to put on.

Chorus So, off she went to her grandfather's tent
And got him some boots of the very very best
She got him some boots of the very very best
And the soldier put them on.

Janet Oh soldier, soldier won't you marry me
With your musket, fife and drum.

Jack Oh no sweet maid I cannot marry you
For I have no hat to put on.

Chorus So, off she went to her grandfather's tent
And got him a hat of the very very best
She got him a hat of the very very best
And the soldier put them on.

By this stage **Jack** *looks utterly ridiculous.* **Rose** *is making faces at him behind his back.* **Vi** *is trying hard not to laugh aloud.* **Dolly** *makes no attempt to conceal her mirth.*

Janet Oh soldier, soldier won't you marry me . . .

She dissolves into laughter. **Jack** *is almost in tears with anger and humiliation. He grabs hold of* **Janet**, *shakes her, shouts.*

Jack Oh no sweet maid I cannot marry you!
For I have a wife of my own!

He runs out.

Back to the present time. **Dolly, Rose, Janet** *and* **Belle** *are laughing at the memory.* **Vi** *looks uncomfortable.*

Belle Oh, I wish I could have seen that. Isn't there a photograph of Jack dressed up?

Dolly You must be jokin'. He run out of here like a scalded cat. Wouldn't speak to any of us for days after.

Vi It wasn't really funny.

Dolly Away on with ye. Ye were laughin' as much as the rest of us.

Did him the world of good. He's always been full of his own importance.

Vi It wasn't easy for him, livin' in a household of women, with no man to . . .

Dolly My Joe was around for a year after he come here to live. I never noticed Jack makin' any effort to enjoy Joe's company. Jack likes to be the *only* man. The one in charge. Thought he'd be the man of the house when Joe died. I soon put him right on that score.

Vi It's gettin' dark. I'll put up the shutters on the shop.

Rose I'll give you a hand.

Dolly An' we'll open a bottle. With any luck Jack'll not turn up an' we can all get bluttered without him sittin' there like Moses makin' the tribe feel guilty.

Vi *and* **Rose** *go to put the steel mesh shutters over the shop windows for the night.*

Rose Why do you always defend him, Vi?

Vi Somebody has to defend him. Everybody needs a friend on their side.

Rose Even when they've done what he's done to Janet?

Vi Have you ever stopped to wonder what their mother and father done to Jack?

Rose They were Janet's parents too, but she's not cruel and vindictive.

Vi You're pretty good at bein' vindictive when it comes to Jack. You never give him a chance. You never liked him from the day and hour he come here.

Rose Do *you* really like him?

Vi He was that lost and lonely, I felt heart sorry for him. Nobody liked him . . . I didn't like him either and I felt bad havin' such feelin's about a child. It's a terrible thing not to like a child. Terrible. I always tried to make it up to him.

Rose By agreeing with his mad religious politics?

Vi I've never been strong on religion, I'm all for people worshippin' as they please. But I've never had to pretend to agree with Jack's politics. I'm with him all the way on that.

Rose No you're not, Vi.

Vi We need somebody strong to speak up for us. To tell the British Government that we won't be handed over to a foreign country without a fight. That we won't be patted on the head and complimented on our loyalty and patriotism through two world wars, but now it's all over, thank you very much, and your loyalty and your patriotism are an embarrassment to us and our American and European allies. We are bein' sold down the river because England doesn't need us no more. An' what we need now is somebody to shout our cause an' our rights from the rooftops. We are as much a part of Great Britain as Liverpool or Manchester or Birmingham. How would they feel if they were suddenly told that the Dublin Government was to have a say in the runnin' of their country!

Rose A third of the population of Northern Ireland were denied a say in how their country should be run.

Vi I've never been opposed to the Catholics havin' their say. Doin' their part. As long as they are prepared to do it with us and not against us. But they've made their position very clear. They don't want to share power. They want to take it.

Rose And the Unionists want to hold on to it. Absolutely. They have to. They will never agree to power sharing because they can't. Northern Ireland was created as a Protestant State for a Protestant People, and if they agree to power sharing, they'll have agreed to do away with the very reason for the state's existence. Don't you see that?

Vi And isn't The South a Catholic State for a Catholic People! You only see what suits you, Rose. And don't try to tell me it would suit you to live in a country where Priests make the laws and tell you how to vote from the altar. Where things like contraception and divorce are a legal and a mortal sin. It's written into their Catholic Constitution. You're a great one for Women's Rights. We wouldn't have many rights in a United Ireland!

Rose We won't have many rights here either, if Jack and his gang get the Independent Ulster they want. Their right-wing Protestant Church is in total agreement with the right-wing Catholic Church on issues like divorce and abortion, on a woman's right to be anything other than a mother or a daughter or a sister or a wife. Any woman outside that set of rules is the Great Whore of Babylon.

One of the first things they'll do if they get their Independent State of Ulster is vote that into their Protestant Constitution.

Vi So, the choice is the devil or the deep blue sea, is that what you're sayin'? Well, in that case I'll stay with the devil I know . . . I don't see why we have to change anything. We were all gettin' on alright before the Civil Rights started the violence. We never had no quarrel with our Catholic neighbours.

Rose There was one Catholic family in this street, and they were intimidated out in 1972.

Vi By strangers. Fly-by-nights from God knows where. Not by the neighbours. Not by us. The Doherty's lived next door for twenty years an' we all got on great. I nursed two of them kids through the measles when their mother was in the hospital havin' her veins done. And she used to come in here regular on the Twelfth of July and help my father put on his Orange Sash for The Parade.

Rose No! That's not true Vi. Bridie Doherty came in here *once* on the Twelfth of July. It was the morning that Granny Dunbar had the stroke, and instead of you and Dolly being here as usual to dress father up for the parade, the two of you were at the hospital. Bridie came in to enquire about Granny, and there father was blundering and bellowing like a bull because he couldn't find his sash.

Vi And Bridie found it behind the sofa and put it round his neck.

Rose She lifted it up and she held it out to him. And suddenly there was a terrible awkwardness between them. She hesitated, and then she placed the sash around his neck.

Vi Like I said.

Rose There was nothing neighbourly or affectionate about it. He was afraid that if he took it out of her hands it would look as if he didn't want a Catholic handling it. And she was afraid that if she set it down again it would look like an insult. That's why she put it round his neck. And then both of them were so uncomfortable and embarrassed that Bridie left without saying a word. That's the truth of what happened. I know, because I was there. I told you that story Vi. And over the years, you and Dolly have romanticized it into something it wasn't.

Vi Better than demeanin' it the way you're now doin'.

Rose Oh Vi. Belfast abounds with half-baked sentimental stories like that. About the good old days and how well we all got on with

our Uncle Tom Catholic neighbours. Sure we did. As long as they stayed indoors on the Twelfth of July and didn't kick up a fuss when the Kick-the-Pope bands marched past their houses, beating big drums to remind them of their place here. The stories are myths. Fables. Distortions of the truth.
Bridie Doherty was the best neighbour we ever had. And what did this family do when the bully boys daubed red paint on her windows and stuffed petrol soaked rags through her letter box!

Vi We put out the fire! We brought them in here! We . . .

Rose We helped them pack and move out.

Vi Now you're distortin' the truth. We didn't want them to go. We wanted them to stay. All the neighbours did. (**Rose** *raises her eyebrows.*) Well, all except that Sinclair clan up the street. But I soon give them a piece of my mind when they started mouthin' about the Dohertys bein' in the I.R.A. Molly Sinclair never said nuthin' like that within earshot of me again, I can tell ye.

Rose Yet you voted for Molly Sinclair's son in the council elections. Head-the-Ball-Harry. Don't be vague. Burn a Tague.

Vi I had no choice. He was the only Unionist Candidate.

Rose You could have voted for one of the more moderate parties.

Vi What! Split the vote and let the Sinn Feiners in? The mouthpiece of bombers and murderers. Sinn Fein. Ourselves Alone. Not much hint of power sharin' in that! Maybe you'd like to see the I.R.A. in control of Belfast City Council.

Rose I'd like to see the people here voting for, and not against, in every election. Sooner or later, Protestant or Catholic, we have all got to take that risk.

Vi We? That's easy to say, when you don't live in the middle of it. When there's no risk of losin' your nationality, your religion, everything you've lived your life by, and believed in.

Dolly (*sings*) In and out the windows
In and out the windows
In and out the windows
As you have done before.

Stand and face your partner
Stand and face your partner
Stand and face your partner

As you have done before.

She pulls a party popper. **Belle** *hands her a drink.*

Dolly (*sings*) Vote vote vote for Maggie Thatcher
In comes Belle at the door, io
For Belle is the one that'll have a bit of fun
And we don't want Maggie any more, io.

As she sings, **Jack** *walks into the street with* **Tom Bailey**. **Bailey** *is middle aged, elegantly dressed, and has a soft cultured British accent. He has the calm self assurance that comes from a life of wealth and privilege. The two men stand for a moment looking at the street and the shop before entering.*

Jack Vi, this is Tom Bailey, the English businessman I mentioned to you last time I was here.

Tom How do you do, Miss Horner. It's a pleasure to meet you.

Vi How do you do, Mr Bailey.

Jack We had hoped to have a quiet word with you . . . alone.

Vi This is my sister Rose.

There is a pause as **Rose** *looks steadily at* **Tom Bailey**. *He smiles and acknowledges the introduction with a slight nod of his head.*

Jack I just called to let you know that I can't come to Dolly's party. I'm taking Tom to the airport after the meeting.

Tom My apologies for this intrusion on a family occasion. I had hoped for the opportunity of an informal private chat, Miss Horner, but it's obviously inconvenient. Perhaps we could arrange to meet later. I'll be back in Belfast in a couple of days.

Rose In time for the Anglo/Irish Protest Rally?

Tom Of course.

Rose What business have you with my sister!

Jack Private business. None of your concern.

Vi Now you just hold on a minute Jack. I don't know what's goin' on here, but anything to do with this house is not goin' to be a dark secret between you and me. It'll be discussed properly by the whole family before any decisions are made. You're rushin' me into somethin' and I don't like it. I never intended to consider this so soon.

Rose Consider what?

Vi I mentioned to Jack one time that I had a mind to move away from here. Take Dolly to end her days somewhere nice and quiet. By the sea maybe. You know she always loved the seaside. Not right now, but maybe in a couple of years or so when I get the pension. I didn't intend so soon . . . so quick . . .

Jack We don't have to discuss this now Vi. We'll call again next week.

Rose Oh no you won't. There is nothing to discuss. This house is not for sale to Tom Bailey as long as I have any say in the matter.

Vi You know this man, Rose?

Rose Let me introduce you properly Vi, to the Reverend Thomas Bailey. Formerly of the Anglican Church, until his Bishop ordered him to sever his connections with the National Front. So Thomas took a leaf from the book of another reverend, Dr Ian Paisley, and formed his own Free Church where no-one had the authority to tell him that all God's children are not necessarily blue eyed, blonde haired and white.

Jack This is outrageous. We don't have to listen to this.

Rose No. But Vi must.

Jack My apologies Tom. I did warn you this would happen if she was here.

Rose (to **Tom**) He knew I would be here. Conceit. Arrogance. You couldn't resist letting me know personally.

Vi How do you know him, Rose?

Rose We met in court when he was prosecuted under the Race Relations Act.

Unlike **Jack, Tom Bailey** *has remained urbane and calm throughout* **Rose***'s outburst.*

Tom Unsuccessfully prosecuted.

Rose His wife, The Lady Elizabeth Montgomery Bailey Q.C. got him acquitted on a legal technicality. When Mrs Bailey isn't in court defending the British right to racism she advises the Ulster Unionists at Westminster on how to break the law within the law in order to keep Northern Ireland Protestant, Orange and White. I wonder Vi, what a well-heeled, upper-crust couple like the Baileys

would be wanting with a huxtery shop and dwelling in a small street
in East Belfast? It's a far cry from their luxury flat in Westminster
and their rolling acres in Surrey.

Tom A purely rhetorical question, Miss Horner. Your sister and
her associates are well informed about my every move.

Rose Not as well as we thought, it would seem. I knew your
associates were looking for premises. I didn't know it would be *you.*
I didn't know it would be *my home.* Was that *your* idea? Does the
notion of operating from my family home appear to your bizarre
sense of humour? Or is it just simple vindictive revenge?

Tom You flatter yourself, Ms Horner. You are not that important.
You made a minor, misguided incursion into my life once. It
scarcely caused a ripple.

Vi Would somebody mind tellin' me what's goin' on here? Jack?

Jack Tom, we must be going. We'll be late.

Tom There is no hurry. The meeting cannot begin without me.
And I have nothing to hide from Miss Horner. Can her sister say
the same?

Rose I have never tried to hide my part in bringing the activities of
you and your family to the attention of the public. In fact I'm
rather proud of those photographs. Some of the best I ever took,
considering the circumstances.

Tom Blurred images from a concealed camera.

Rose Not so blurred that you and those other wealthy aristocratic
Fascists in Nazi uniforms, couldn't be identified.

Tom A man may dress as he pleases in the privacy of his own
home.

Rose But not in the privacy of mine!

Vi What has all this to do with my shop?

Rose Mr Bailey doesn't parade publicly through the streets with
the National Front. He's much too refined for that. But he does
provide them with advice, legal assistance, money, meeting places.
They're planning to open an H.Q. in Belfast. A twenty four hour
service for the faithful. A shop outlet for their propaganda. Back
rooms for meetings. They've been here quietly for years.
Observing. Participating. One of their leaders recently described

Northern Ireland as the perfect springboard for their activities in the United Kingdom. They're now confident enough to crawl out of the woodwork, and go public.

Tom I have always had confidence in the loyalty of the Protestant people of Ulster.

Rose The type of loyalty you're talking about is of *some* of the Protestant people. Not *all* of the Protestant people. And not nearly as many as Paisley claims.

Tom You are mistaken Ms Horner. You represent a very small minority. Without support. Without power.

Jack She is also, as ever, a deceiver. Even as a child you delighted in knowing and telling other people's secrets while being close about your own. Vi asked a question and you answer it with exaggerated gossip about why Tom Bailey is here, but carefully avoid mentioning why you are here.

Vi Rose?

Rose This week I am here for the pure pleasure of being with my family. Next week I won't be going back to England with Belle. I'll be moving into the Europa Hotel to work with two colleagues, journalists, who are here investigating the links between the National Front, The British Friends of Ulster, and the Democratic Unionist Party.

Vi You were plottin' to stay on in Belfast and not say?

Rose There was no plot Vi. I happened to have a free week when Belle was on half term holiday, and it was a perfect opportunity to come home with her. The fact that I have a job here next week is coincidental.

Vi Oh, I see. If you hadn't happened to be free this week, you would have sneaked into a Belfast hotel next week, without even lettin' the family know you were in the city?

Rose Yes. I would. Partly because it's business and it's confidential. But mainly, because it would be too risky to work from home. John Horner may be safe in the arms of Tom Bailey, but John Horner's cousins are not safe from abusive phone calls and threatening letters and other tactics of the violence Tom Bailey funds. I couldn't risk exposing you and Dolly to the possibility of that.

Tom I would commend your concern about your family Ms

Horner if I didn't know how willingly you have already exposed
them to possible risk in your determination to discredit your cousin
John Horner. However, I suppose the betrayal of one's family is a
minor consideration in one so ready to betray one's country.

Rose What country would that be, Mr Bailey?

Tom England. Ulster.

Rose You are as ill-informed as most of the English about this
country. This is Northern Ireland, not Ulster. Not Donegal, Cavan
and Monaghan. The so-called Ulster Unionists gave those areas
with a Catholic majority to the South in 1920 in order to create and
maintain their own false majority.

Tom I see you've been reading your daughter's history books. I
hear she's quite an intelligent student, despite her antecedents . . .
and despite a rather dangerous tendency to support somewhat
suspect left wing causes . . .

Vi (*very quietly*). Get out of this house.

Jack Vi . . .

Vi Makin' threats about Belle . . .

Jack Tom didn't intend . . .

Vi I know a threat when I hear one. Even when it's made by a well
spoken gentleman. And nobody threatens our Belle, nobody! She's
my sister's child with the same ancestors as me. She's my niece and
your cousin. She's family, and by the looks of things, the only
grandchild this family's likely to have.

Jack She's not family! She's . . .

Rose A black bastard?

Jack If the cap fits . . .

Rose She's a blood relation of yours whether you like it or not,
Jack. Or maybe first cousins once removed don't count with your
chums in the National Front?

Jack Why should I be considered responsible for your ungodly
fornications.

He walks out.

Rose If you're going to join the war here Thomas Bailey, never
forget that loyalty to one's immediate family will always take

precedence over loyalty to the Unionist family.

Tom I'll bear that in mind.

Rose You do that. Ireland has been the death of better Englishmen than you.

He smiles and leaves unhurriedly.

Pause. **Vi** *and* **Rose** *just look at each other.*

Rose Thanks Vi.

Vi For what! For defendin' Belle? Or for havin' the fall-out with Jack that you've been engineerin' ever since you were a child! You never could leave well alone could you? You were an indulged brat when you were wee and you haven't changed one whit. Still stirrin' it. Always gettin' away with it. A pretty face. A clever tongue. Father always said you could charm the birds off the trees. 'Look after Rose, Vi. She's our wee flower.' He never had a pet name for me. Good old Vi. Martha to your Mary. Vi'll make the dinner while Rose is makin' daydreams. No matter what I did for him he always took it for granted. No more than was his due. God, he had it made. A wife to play act for him. A little daughter to pet and indulge. And a dutiful dependable grown-up daughter to cook his meals and starch his shirts.

Rose Don't Vi. Don't. You always loved him so. He loved you.

Vi Aye. Because I deserved it. But he adored you regardless. *He* adored you. *Dolly* adored you. *Everybody* adored you. (*Pause,* **Rose** *is very shaken that* **Vi** *might be about to say she hated her.* **Vi** *continues more quietly.*) *I* adored you. Silly oul maid. Pushing you round the park in that great Silver Cross pram they bought when you were born. 'Nothing's too good for our Rose.' Strangers used to stop and compliment me on my beautiful baby. And I let them assume you were mine. I expect they also assumed you got your good looks from my husband. Not from a plain lump like me. I used to get into these terrible panics in case one of them would happen to come into the shop and discover that you were really my sister, and tell Dolly about my foolishness. And then she would have told father and they would have laughed together in that close way of theirs as if they were the only two people in the world.

Rose I'm sorry Vi. I don't know what else to say. Except that, if you and I had never been born, they would still have been totally happy, just the two of them.

Vi I know. (*Pause.*) Why have you never got married Rose?

Rose Why haven't you? And don't say you were never asked, because I know you were.

Vi Nosy wee bitch. I knew you were listenin' at the door. He's an assistant manager in the Ulster Bank now. If I'd played my cards right, I could be livin' in a split-level bungalow in Holywood, Co. Down.

Rose And I could be singing hymns in a Baptist Church in America.

Vi Maybe it's just as well that growin' up with the real thing made us both too choosy, eh?

Belle *comes in.*

Belle Gran says if you two don't come in this minute, she's starting the party without you.

Vi Since when did Dolly ever need the go-ahead to start a party? You go in and monitor her drink allowance, Rose. Belle, you give me a hand with the shutters.

Belle *carries the shutters outside.*

Vi Don't let her go to the rally.

Rose Don't worry. I'll talk to her later. (*Pause.*) I love you Vi.

Vi I love you too. Even if you are the most thrawn child this family has ever known.

Vi *goes outside.*

Rose *goes to* **Dolly** *and* **Janet.**

Dolly One down. Two to go.

Rose They're putting up the shutters. They won't be a minute.

Dolly You and Vi have had enough time to put shutters round the Great Wall of China. What's been goin' on out there?

Rose Jack's been and gone. He won't be back for the party.

Dolly That's the best bit of news there's been since the relief of Derry.

Janet Do you want a drink, Rose?

Rose Yes, please.

Dolly Here, top mine up while you're at it.

Rose Take it easy. You know what the doctor said.

Dolly You're a long time dead. Here (*Holding out the photo album.*) Remember this one. It was the time you an' Janet got saved down in the mission hall by that buck eejit Issac Standaloft and his sister Naomi.

Janet (*to* **Rose**). Remember? We only went down in the first place because we'd heard about Naomi crossing her hands when she played the piano.

Dolly God, the way that woman murdered a good tune wasn't ordinary.

Dolly *sings (badly) and mimes* **Naomi Standaloft** *playing the piano with exaggerated gestures. Sound of a piano.*

As **Dolly** *sings, she becomes* **Naomi.**

Janet *and* **Rose** *join in as ten year olds. They are torn between giggling and fascination at* **Naomi**'s *elaborate playing.*

Dolly (*sings*) Climb climb up Sunshine Mountain
Singing as we go.
Climb climb up Sunshine Mountain
Faces all aglow.
Turn turn your back on Satan
Look up to the sky
Climb climb up Sunshine Mountain
You and I.

She shouts 'all together now!' and **Rose** *and* **Janet** *sing the song and march around the room. As they finish, the preacher* **Issac Standaloft** *walks on. He is a plump perspiring man in an ill fitting suit. He has a north of England accent.* **Naomi** *heralds his arrival with a fanfare on the piano.* **Issac** *stands for a moment, eyes shut, a tortured expression on his face.* **Naomi** *goes to him and comforts him.*

Issac Behold a pearl among women. My dear devoted sister Naomi. But for her faith and goodness I, Issac Standaloft, would still be sliding down the slippery slopes, towards the fires of Hell! I was a bad child, corrupted by the unholy passions of Satan's cinemas. I became a dissipated youth who forsook his Christian home for the drinking dens of the Devil and the dreadful desires of women who dance! Be not like them. The Devil's voluptuous temptresses with painted faces and lacquered nails and hair dyed red with sin. Beware of the devil who lurks in the dark dance halls and hostelrys and picture palaces. He wants your youth. He wants your bodies. He wants your souls.

Be as Naomi. Be unadorned. Be modest. Be chaste. Be not the foul instrument of the downfall of men. Your souls belong to God. Your bodies are his temple. Only your lawful wedded husband may worship and enter therein, not for pleasure, but purely for the procreation of God's children. But first, you must cleanse that temple of the original sin of your worldly birth. Ye must be saved. Ye must be born again. You must, or you will surely face the fiery furnace and burn forever. Come on to me. Come on to me, before it is too late.

Naomi, *who has been gazing at* **Issac** *with ecstatic passion brings the two children forward.*

Isaac *embraces* **Naomi, Janet** *and* **Rose**. *There are sexual overtones in how he touches them.*

Issac Sing Naomi! Sing!

Dolly/Naomi (*sing*) There is one thing I will not do
I will not stand in a cinema queue

Isaac and Naomi There is one thing I will not do
I will not stand in a cinema queue
I ain't a gonna grieve my Lord no more

Naomi All together now!

All I ain't a gonna grieve my Lord
I ain't a gonna grieve my Lord
I ain't a gonna grieve my Lord no more.

Issac There are two things

Naomi There are two things

Issac I do detest

Naomi I do detest.

Issac A painted face

Naomi A painted face

Issac And a low backed dress

Naomi And a low backed dress

All There are two things I do detest

A painted face and a low backed dress
I ain't a gonna grieve my Lord no more
I ain't a gonna grieve my Lord
I ain't a gonna grieve my Lord
I ain't a gonna grieve my Lord no more.

Issac There are three things

All There are three things

Issac I will not do

All I will not do

Issac I will not gamble, smoke nor chew

All There are three things I will not do
I will not gamble, smoke nor chew
I ain't a gonna grieve my Lord no more
I ain't a gonna grieve my Lord
I ain't a gonna grieve my Lord
I ain't a gonna grieve my Lord no more.

During the singing of the last chorus, **Issac** *and* **Naomi** *dance off.* **Rose** *and* **Janet** *sit down and look pious. They sing a few bars of 'Sunshine Mountain' without much enthusiasm.* **Dolly** *returns (as herself). She takes a photo of them. She shakes her head in exasperation.*

Dolly Tell me this an' tell me no more! How long are the pair of ye plannin' to keep up this daft carry-on? I mean, I can cope with a couple of ten year olds not boozin' nor gamblin' nor smokin' nor frequentin' the Plaza Ballroom. But I declare to God if I hear one more chorus about climbin' up that friggin' Sunshine Mountain it's the friggin' Sunshine Home for Wayward Girls for you two before this day's over. Now away out to the street and play with the other kids an' give my head peace.

Janet There's nobody to play with. They're all away to the pictures

Rose (*wistfully*). It's Lassie, so it is. An' Bugs Bunny.

Dolly What time does it start?

Janet Two o'clock.

Dolly I think I'll go an' see that. He's great crack that oul Bugs Bunny. (**Janet** *and* **Rose** *watch with mounting anguish as* **Dolly** *prepares to go.*) If I rush I'll see the comin' attractions as well. I hear A Hundred and One Dalmatians is on next week. Now how much money do I have on me . . . (*She looks in her purse.*) Enough for three an' a bit over for choc ices . . . pity ye can't come with me. Still, yiz can say a wee prayer for me while I'm away sinnin'.

She moves towards the door. **Janet** *and* **Rose** *look at each other.*

Rose That oul Issac Standaloft's a smelly pervert, so he is.

She runs after **Dolly.**

Janet Wait for me! Wait for me!

She runs to **Dolly** *and* **Rose.** **Dolly** *links a child on each arm. They exit with* **Dolly** *singing 'Onward Christian Soldiers'.*

Scene Two

The morning of the protest rally.

Vi *carries the steel shutters from outside into the shop.*

Rose *comes in from the house.*

Rose What are you doing?

Vi What does it look like I'm doin'?

Rose You're opening the shop?

Vi No. I'm takin' up weight liftin' in my old age. Here, prop that behind the counter instead of standin' there with both your arms the same length.

Rose I thought you were supporting the strike.

Vi Well you thought wrong. I'm in support of the protest, but I'm gettin' out of the corner they've boxed us into. 'Close your shop, an' take to the streets if you don't support The Agreement.' I will never support that agreement, never. But neither will I be a part of what they've got us involved in. Civil disobedience aided and abetted by thugs. Them's I.R.A. tactics, an' I'll have no part of it. I've paid my rates, despite their orders not to. I've never been in debt in my life, an' I won't start now.

Rose Vi, I never intended this . . .

Vi I'm not doin' it for you. I'm doin' it for me. And well dare anybody round here suggest I'm not as loyal as the next one. I'm

British, an' that's what I'll fight to stay as long as there's breath in my body. But I'll do it respectably and with dignity. I won't be associated with the dictates of criminals.

Rose I should be at home today.

Vi No. Your place is with the rest of the media who've congregated here, hopin' there's goin' to be a riot this day.

Rose I don't hope that.

Vi Maybe not. But the rest of them surely do. A peaceful protest is no news.

Belle *comes in.*

Vi What are you doin' up at this hour of the mornin'?

Belle I want to get into town early. Get near the front. See the speakers.

Rose You are not going to the rally.

Belle I am going to the rally. It's a historical happening. When I get back to college, I can tell those dusty old history lecturers that while they've been reading about it, I've been there.

Vi You can watch it on the six o'clock news. You'll get a better view. And a safer one.

Belle I'll be alright. Davy has promised to hold my hand.

Vi The blind leadin' the blind. You said you would talk to her, Rose.

Rose I did talk to her. (*To* **Belle**.) Weren't you listening to a word I said!

Belle I listened. And I've thought about it. And I want to go to the rally. I'm not afraid of the National Front.

Rose Well I am. And I'm telling you to stay indoors today.

Belle You can't tell me what to do. I'm eighteen. And I don't live at home anymore. I can fight my own battles.

Rose I have worked day and night since you were born to make sure that you've never had to fight this battle. You've never known what it's like to be hated because you are black. I have kept you safe, well clear of poor, violent streets and schools, and . . .

Belle And now you want to live my life for me?

Rose I didn't give you a life to see it destroyed on the streets of Belfast. Now stop being silly.

Belle And you stop being so melodramatic!

Vi Hey, hey, calm down the pair of you.

Rose It's always the same. I talk to her. I'm reasonable. She's not. She just goes off quietly and does whatever it was she decided to do in the first place.

Vi I wonder who she takes that after? (*To* **Belle**.) Listen love. We're both worried. Nobody's tryin' to lead your life for you. We just don't want you to come to no harm.

Pause.

Belle The National Front are recent arrivals here. Like me. Why have I never been in Belfast before now?

Vi It was always easier for Dolly and me to visit you than for Rose to bring a baby across the water. Dolly loved them trips.

Belle I haven't been a baby for a long time.

Rose I couldn't afford the fare. You don't remember our early days in London. The rotten rooms we lived in before I began to earn decent money.

Belle You've had a well paid job for as long as I *can* remember, and you've taken me all over the world with you. But never to Belfast. One hour away by plane. So if it wasn't the time and it wasn't the money, what was the reason?

Rose Belle love, what is all this about?

Belle You haven't protected me from racism you know. No amount of money can buy immunity from that. But I've always dealt with it in my own way. Quietly. Never told you because you're always too anxious to fight on my behalf.

Rose You're my daughter.

Belle You're not black. I am. You can decide not to be a Protestant. I can't decide not to be black. I have no problem about being black. Is it a problem to you?

Rose What are you saying?

Belle I don't know. (*Pause.*) I'm saying that I'm not as concerned about political issues like the National Front, as I am by the thought that you . . . this family . . . might have been embarrassed by me. Maybe still are.

Rose How could you think such a thing.

Belle I don't know. Didn't realize it was in my head until I said it. And now I've said it and I wish I hadn't. Don't look at me like that. I feel bad enough already.

Rose And so you should.

Vi Better sayin' it than harbourin' it. And she has a right to know.

Rose There's nothing to know.

Vi Oh come on Rose. You know as well as I do, that although we never sat down and discussed it, we came to an unspoken agreement that it would be easier all round if me and Dolly visited you and Belle instead of you comin' here and copin' with the waggin' tongues. (*To* **Belle**.) Bein' an unmarried mother was scandal enough here all them years ago, but havin' a black child was unheard of. We may say we meant it for the best, but it's not to our credit that we took the easy way out at first, and then over the years just let it go on that way. If I'm ashamed of anything it's us. Not you. The very idea! I couldn't love you more if you were my own. So no more daft notions! All right madam?

Belle I'm sorry.

Vi I should think so indeed.

Pause.

Belle So I wasn't a dark family secret then?

Vi Aye, you were. For all of a fortnight, 'til I got back from London laden with photos. Dolly was that ashamed of you she pinned the lot up behind the counter, and bored the entire street to death boastin' about you. It's a wonder she didn't take out a full page advert in the Belfast Telegraph.

Belle I'm sorry. I won't ever think it again.

Vi You'd better not. And to make amends you can stay and help me run the shop today.

Belle Janet's here. I could go in with *you*, mum. Then you wouldn't need to worry about me.

Rose No. This is not an outing. This is work. And I'm late. But I'm not going in until I have your promise that you won't go in on your own.

Belle It's not fair!

Rose Please Belle. This is one crowd I don't want you standing out in.

Belle (*reluctantly*) Alright.

Rose Promise.

Belle I promise. Okay?

Rose Thank you. I'll get back as soon as I can. Take care Vi.

Vi You too.

Rose *leaves.*

Belle Do you want me to make the sandwiches?

Vi No point. Nobody'll be in to buy them.

Belle Then why bother opening. We could go in to Belfast together. I only promised mum I wouldn't go in alone.

Vi Your mother did not say, don't go in alone. She said, don't go in on your own. Meanin' off your own bat. Under your own steam. With or without company.

Belle That's not how I understood it.

Vi Oh is it not, clever clogs. Well the answer is still no. I've made up my mind to open the day, an' I won't be deterred. Not even by the big brown eyes of the Belle of the Belfast City. Now you just content yourself and keep an eye on the shop while I get Dolly up and dressed. I'll send Janet down to keep you company and out of mischief.

Vi *moves towards the house.*

Belle Vi?

Vi What?

Belle Are you opening the shop, making a stand, just because of me? I mean . . . would you feel so strongly about the National Front being here, if I were white?

Vi After the second world war, your grandfather sent me and Dolly to the pictures to see the newsreels of what had been goin' on in them camps in Germany. He was there, when they were liberated, you see, an' he said everybody should see what he'd seen, an' never forget it, so that it could never happen again. He was a good man. A decent man. I wish you could have known him. He would have spoilt you rotten. He would never have condoned the followers of them butchers marchin' on the streets of Belfast. And neither will I.

She goes upstairs. There is the sound of bands in the road near the street. **Belle** *goes out to look.* **Davy** *comes into the street. He is wearing even more red, white and blue badges and Loyalist slogans than usual. He has an 'Ulster Says No' poster taped to the back of his coat. He signals excitedly to* **Belle**, *miming the bands and telling her to come with him.*

Belle I can't Davy ... I promised ... (*She hesitates then signals.*) Hold on a minute. I'll get my coat.

She puts on a coat. Scribbles a note to **Vi**. *Leaves it on the counter. She holds out her hand to* **Davy**. *He smiles shyly and takes it. The noise of the bands increases.*

As **Belle** *and* **Davy** *leave the street,* **Janet** *comes in to the shop. She reads the note, grabs her coat and runs after them.*

Scene Three

Late afternoon the same day. A room in Unionist Party headquarters. **Jack** *stands rehearsing a speech. At first he refers occasionally to his notes but by the end of the speech he is in a state of masturbatory ecstasy.*

Jack Today, the internal feuding within the Unionist Family is ended. No longer divided, we shall not fall. Strong and re-united we stand. Unafraid in the face of our common enemy. We are at war with the British Government, and our ranks will never be broken again. We will never submit to the conspiracy of the Anglo-Irish Agreement. Fight the Good Fight. Rejoice in your strength. But beware of complacency. For therein lies weakness. And weakness may be seduced by that other great conspiracy – the corruption and perfidy of Rome.

Be constantly on your guard against the satanic smells and heathen incantations that pervade the Roman Catholic Church. The descendant Church of the Semitic God Baal. Baal the Sun God. Baal the Master. Baal the Possessor. Baal the Seducer.

Guard our women. Guard our children. Lest they succumb to the insidious evil that festers and grows in our land. The phallic worship of priests in scarlet and gold. The pagan rites of black nuns. Sisters of satan. Sisters of sin. Defilers of man's .

Guard your mothers. Guard your daughters. Guard your sisters and your wives.

And may God guard us lest we weaken and yield to Unholy Desire.

Janet *comes in.*

There is a long pause.

Janet They said I would find you here.

Jack I gave instructions that I was not to be disturbed.

Janet I told them I was your sister. I have to talk to you.

Jack You'll have to wait. I'm about to address a meeting.

Janet This can't wait. I need your help.

Jack So. You've come to your senses at last.

Janet It's not for me. It's for Davy.

Jack Who?

Janet Davy Watson. You've met him in the shop. He's deaf and dumb.

Jack What about him?

Janet He's been arrested and I can't find out where they've taken him.

Jack Ask your policeman.

Janet Peter's on duty. I don't know where.

Jack I've more important things to do than wander round the police stations looking for a halfwit.

Janet I'll tell Vi I asked for your help and that's what you said.

Jack Wait. Tell me what happened.

Janet He went to the rally with Belle. She was told not to go, but she was determined to see it for herself. I went after them, but there was no stopping her.

Jack Every inch her mother's daughter. Disobedient and defiant.

Janet I couldn't talk her out of it, so I went with them. On the way home, we were stopped by a crowd of kids wearing National Front teeshirts. Five boys and two girls. The girls were wearing Union Jacks around their shoulders. Like cloaks. They couldn't have been more than fourteen years old.

Jack Will you get on with it. I haven't got all night.

Janet They made a circle round Belle. Started taunting her, pushing her about, pulling her hair. Davy went berserk. Dived on them like a madman. A police patrol came along and the kids ran away. All that was left was me and Belle trying to calm Davy down. The police assumed he was attacking us, and dragged him into the landrover. We tried to explain to them, but they weren't interested. One of them kept shouting about a colleague who'd been injured earlier on at the City Hall. I suppose they were determined to get somebody. Anybody. Then something came through on the radio and they drove off. Belle and me have been everywhere, Jack, and nobody will give us any information. So we came here.

Jack You've brought her here!

Janet She's outside. In a taxi.

Jack Go home! I'll make some phone calls.

Janet Belle says she's not going home without him.

Jack Tell her to clear off from here, or I'll leave him to rot!

Janet Can you get him out?

Jack We still have some friends in the R.U.C. Influential men. Not community do-gooders like your husband.

Janet I no longer have a husband.

Pause.

Jack You will always have a brother.

Janet Goodbye Jack.

She turns to leave.

Jack You need me!

Janet I never needed you. I was only ever afraid of your need of me. And now I'm not afraid any more.

Jack What are you going to do! Live out your days with that mad old woman? She's already got one foot in the grave. She won't last for ever. And Vi's not getting any younger. What'll you do when they're both gone! You'll never manage alone. You never could. You've always needed somebody to take care of you.

Janet It's time I took care of myself. I'm going to London.

Jack You met a man there, didn't you? Didn't you!

Janet Yes I did. But I'm not running back to him. I want a life of my own. My own! Nobody else's! Not his, not Peter's. Not yours. Most of all not yours. I am walking away from this violence.

Jack I am not a violent man. I abhor violence.

Janet You love it, Jack. You need it. It excites you. Violence is the woman you never had.

Jack I need no woman.

Janet Then you don't need me.

She walks away.

Jack (*shouts after her*) I have never needed you! Harlot! Whore!

Dolly (*sings*) Let him go let him tarry
Let him sink or let him swim.
He doesn't care for me
And I don't care for him.
He can go and get another
That I hope he will enjoy.
For I'm goin' to marry a far nicer boy.

Janet *walks away into Scene Four.*

Scene Four

Evening. The same day.

Dolly, Vi, Rose, Janet *and* **Belle** *in the house.*

Vi There were two of them. A young lad of about fifteen and a middle aged man. The boy was loud-mouthed, abusive, every other word a swear word. The man was quiet spoken. Quite reasonable I suppose. In his own way. He sent the boy outside and then he talked to me about the agreement and how we all had to oppose it. When I pointed out that the organizers had promised there would be be no intimidation, he said there would be no damage done to the shop, but that it would be boycotted if I didn't close. After he left I put the shutters back on the windows. Just as well, as it turned out. They started comin' back from the rally in the late afternoon. A gang of them. Singin'. Shoutin'. I thought it was stones they were throwin'. It was golf balls.

Janet They smashed in the windows of a sports shop near the city hall. They used the golf balls to attack the police. The owner of that shop is a Protestant business man. He'd closed his premises. But that didn't deter them.

Rose They wrecked and looted about a dozen shops. They were very selective in what they stole. Alcohol. Leather jackets. Ski anoraks. I got a great photograph of one young boy walking around with a bottle of champagne in each hand and a pair of ski boots round his neck.

Dolly Maybe the U.D.A. are plannin' to open a ski resort in the Mourne Mountains.

Belle Was that a car?

Jack *walks into the street with* **Davy**. *He brings him into the house.* **Davy** *is in a distressed, confused state.*

Jack I don't know where he lives, and he couldn't tell me, so I brought him here.

Belle *and* **Vi** *try to comfort* **Davy**. *But he cowers and whimpers and won't let them touch him.*

Vi In the name of God what have they done to him.

Belle It's alright Davy, it's alright. (**Davy** *signals that she is not to come near.*) I won't touch you. I won't come near. I promise. just talk to me. Tell me.

After a pause, **Davy** *signals and Belle interprets.*

Belle They put me in a room. No windows. Bright light. No toilet. They laughed. They made me take my clothes off. All of them. Cold. Cold. They gave me an old blanket. Pushing. Shouting. Shoving. Bright light. Stop. Don't. Cry-baby. Cry . . . I couldn't help it. It wouldn't stop. Dirty. All over the blanket. Don't laugh . . . don't laugh . . . Don't . . . They put the blanket over my head. (**Davy** *touches his hair, looks at his hands with disgust.*) Don't touch. Don't touch . . .

He rocks back and forward, weeping.

Vi Come on, son. Come with me. It doesn't matter. It'll wash off. I'll fill a bath for you. Come on now. You don't want to be going home to your mother in that state. Don't worry. It'll all wash away, and nobody need ever know. We won't tell it. Come on now.

She leads **Davy** *off.* **Dolly** *and* **Janet** *have been watching and listening to the story with horror.* **Rose** *has been watching* **Jack***.*

Rose But you'll tell it, won't you Jack. What a godsend to distract attention from the violence of your gangsters today. I can just see the headline. 'Brutal R.U.C. interrogation of innocent, retarded loyalist'. A heaven-sent piece of propaganda in your favour.

Jack You think they should be allowed to get away with it?

Rose No I don't. No more than I thought they should have been allowed to get away with it when they did that and worse during the interrogation of suspected I.R.A. terrorists. But that never bothered the Unionists at all, did it? In fact you were all for it, as long as it was being done to the Catholics, innocent or guilty.

Jack They're all guilty. Potential traitors every one.

Belle Regardless of what your motives are, I'm grateful to you for getting Davy out of there.

Jack I did it for Vi, because she cares for him and I care about her. But as for the rest of this family, you can all go to hell!

Dolly I doubt there'll be much room left down there. It must be packed out with the clergy by now. (*She grins as* **Jack** *turns angrily to leave. She chants.*) Two little sausages frying in the pan. One went pop and the other went bang.

She starts to laugh and then falls forward out of the chair. **Belle** *runs to* **Dolly***, cradles her in her arms.*

Rose Janet! Phone for an ambulance!

Dolly No ambulance . . . no hospital . . . my own time . . .

Jack *pushes* **Belle** *aside as* **Dolly** *stops breathing. He very expertly begins to resuscitate her.*

Belle Leave her alone! Leave her alone!

Rose Belle!

She restrains **Belle** *from pulling* **Jack** *away.*

Belle Make him stop! She doesn't want this! Let her go! Let her go!

Jack She's breathing again. Put a blanket over her, keep her warm.

Belle Who taught you to do that! The Church Lads Brigade! Why couldn't you leave her alone! I promised her! I promised her! People have the right to die when they want to. When their time has come.

Jack That is for the Lord God to decide.

Belle And you're the Lord God, are you?

Jack I am the instrument of his will.

Belle So were the thumbscrews and the rack.

Janet The ambulance is on its way.

Belle I'm sorry gran . . . I'm sorry . . .

Scene Five

A few months later. A 'sold' sign on the shop.

Dolly *sits in the wheelchair. She looks very old. Vacant. Her mouth is slightly twisted. Some knitting lies in her lap.* **Vi** *is packing things in cardboard boxes.*

Belle *sits on a suitcase at one side of the stage.* **Rose** *and* **Janet** *stand a little way off.* **Janet** *is looking at a newspaper.*

Vi We got a fair price for the shop. Better than I expected. I suppose I should have guessed. It sold so quick. She seemed a nice young woman. Paid cash. Transpired Tom Bailey put up the money, and as soon as it was all signed, sealed and delivered, she transferred the deeds into his name. Rose says he's buyin' up property all over the town. It's one of the ways he makes his money. Buyin' cheap an' waitin' an' sellin' dear. I suppose in the end that's what it all boils down to. Property. Land, who owns what. God, would you listen to me. Next thing, I'll be votin' for the Workers' Party.

She gives **Dolly** *a drink out of a child's plastic cup with a lid and spout.*

Vi You'll love the wee house in Donaghadee. You can see the sea

and the Copeland Islands and the lighthouse. And the girls are
comin' over from London to help us pack up and move. It'll be just
like the old days, only better . . . and you'll get better. It'll take time
. . . but you will . . . (*She picks up the knitting.*) Encourage her to knit
the doctor said. It'll help to get those hands working again. You
never knit nor sewed nothin' in your life, did you mother. I
suppose it's a bit late in the day to expect you to learn new tricks.
(*She puts the photo album on **Dolly**'s lap.*) Here, look at the pictures.
Turn the pages. That'll do your hands and your heart more good.

Dolly *stares at the album. Slowly turns the pages.*

Davy *comes running in. He is wearing an expensive ski anorak and
waving a local magazine. He signals to **Vi** to look, points to a photograph,
points to himself.*

Vi Calm down. Calm down. I can see it's you. I'd know that ugly
mug anywhere. (*She reads.*) British barrister to represent loyalist
victim of R.U.C. brutality. I hope the Lady Elizabeth has been
forewarned to advise you not to appear in court in that jacket. Fell
off the back of a protest lorry, did it? How much did they sting ye
for it? (**Davy** *signals.*) A tenner? Was that with or without golf balls?

Janet *reads to **Rose** from the newspaper.*

Janet Mr David Watson is deaf and dumb and has a mental age of
ten. Mr Jack Horner announced today that he would be Mr
Watson's voice in court. Mr Horner said that he had learned sign
language specially to communicate with Mr Watson who is an old
family friend.

Rose Suffer the little children to come unto me . . . for of such is
the Kingdom of Heaven . . .

Davy *shows the magazine to **Dolly**.*

Vi He's got his photo in the magazine, and there's a write up . . . .
She's not herself the day, Davy. Come back the marra and see her
eh? Maybe she'll be a bit brighter.

Davy *signals goodbye. As he leaves he makes a victory sign and then signals
again.*

Vi (*to **Dolly***). He says 'No Pope Here' (*She shakes her head as **Davy**
exits.*) No bloody wonder son. No bloody wonder.

Dolly *stares at the concert hall poster.* **Belle** *sings.*

Belle Red brick in the suburbs, white horse on the wall

Eyetalian marble in the City Hall
O stranger from England, why stand so aghast?
May the Lord in his mercy be kind to Belfast.

This jewel that houses our hopes and our fears
Was knocked up from the swamp in the last hundred years
But the last shall be first and the first shall last.
May the Lord in his mercy be kind to Belfast.

We swore by King William there'd never be seen
An all-Irish Parliament at College Green
So to Stormont we're nailing the flag to the mast
May the Lord in his mercy be kind to Belfast.

O the bricks they will bleed and the rain it will weep
And the damp Lagan fog lull the city to sleep
It's to hell with the future and live on the past
May the Lord in his mercy be kind to Belfast.

Did You Hear The One About The Irishman . . .?

A Love Story

For Richard Howard

Did You Hear The One About The Irishman . . ? was given a rehearsed reading by the Royal Shakespeare Company in America in 1985. It was first performed at the King's Head Theatre, London in 1987 with the following cast:

Allison Clarke	Janet Behan
Brian Rafferty	John Keegan
The Comedian	Richard Howard
Mrs Boyd **Mrs Clarke** **Bernie Cassidy** }	Jane Lowe
Mr Clarke **The Irishman/Newsreader** }	Ultan Ely O'Carroll
Hugie Boyde **Joe Rafferty** }	Billy Clarke
Marie Rafferty	Mandy MᶜIlwaine

Director	Caroline Sharman
Designer	Angus Campbell
Lighting Design	Steve O'Brien
Stage Manager	Mark Jones
Production Assistant	Lauren Emmerson

Belfast 1987

Irishman (*reading from a list*) Her Majesty's Prison, Maze, Lisburn,
Northern Ireland, 1987. Permitted Christmas Parcels for H/Blocks.
25 small cigars (cigarette size) or 100 cigarettes or 4 and a half oz.
tobacco.
2lb chocolates or sweets. 2lb cake quartered.
2lb loose biscuits.
One unstuffed chicken, boned and quartered.
1lb sliced cooked meat.
4lb Fresh Fruit – No bananas or pears.

Spotlight on the **Comedian**. *He tells jokes directly to the audience as if he is
performing in a club. The* **Irishman** *stops reading the list as his voice is
drowned by the* **Comedian***'s voice. He watches the comedy routine
impassively.*

Comedian Good morning everyone. This is your captain speaking.
We are now approaching the city of Belfast. Will all passengers
please fasten their seatbelts and turn their watches back three
hundred years.
The time is seven a.m. And if there are any Irish passengers on
board, that means that the big hand is at twelve and the little hand
is at seven.
Did you hear the one about the Irishman whose plane ran out of
peat? He radioed for help. Mayday! Mayday!

'Cleared to land', answered Control, 'Can you give us your height and position?'

'Certainly, said the Irishman, 'I'm five foot two and I'm sitting at the front of the plane.' Then there was the Irish terrorist whose first assignment was to hijack an aeroplane. It turned out to be his last assignment. As soon as the plane took off he lit the fuse, put the bomb under his seat, and told the captain that everybody had three minutes to get out.

Little Paddy heard the story and it made him very nervous about flying. So he always carried a bomb in his suitcase every time he had to travel by plane. He figured that the chances of two people on the same flight carrying a bomb were practically nil.

The **Comedian** *pauses to drink some beer.*

Irishman Individual Christmas parcels. Maze Prison. Compound Seventeen. 400 Cigarettes or 12 oz. tobacco or 25 small cigars.
6 mince pies.
One fruit loaf – 1lb.
6 Pastries.
6 Baps.
1lb Chocolates.
2lb Sweets.
3lb Christmas Cake with no marzipan.

The Rafferty House. 7am.

Brian Rafferty *and his sister* **Marie** *are packing a food parcel for their brother* **Joe** *who is in the Maze Prison.*

Brian You know, a committee of grown men must have sat round a table and compiled these lists and decided that marzipan was a threat to national security.

Marie Where are you going?

Brian I'm going to phone Allison.

Marie You'll finish this first!

Brian I'll finish it when I've phone Allison.

He goes to the phone.

Marie She'll be the finish of you, that one.

Comedian An Irish telephonist answered an international call. It's a long distance from America, said the operator. Sure any fool knows that, said the Irish telephonist, and hung up.

Irishman Bulk Christmas Parcels. Maze Prison. Compound 17.
2 large tins of coffee.
5 turkeys cooked and stuffed.
8lb sausages, cooked.
2 mince pies per prisoner.
2 pastries per prisoner – small bun size.
8 cakes not over 2lb. each.
12 christmas puddings not over 2lb. each.
3 christmas trees maximum 4ft. 6 inches.
No decorations. Prisoners to buy them from the tuck shop. All
parcels to be signed.

Comedian (*to the* **Irishman**) Have you heard the latest Irish joke?

Irishman I'm warning you. I'm an Irishman myself.

Comedian That's all right Paddy. I'll tell it nice and slowly for you.

The Clarke House 7am.

Allison *sitting waiting for* **Brian** *to call. The phone rings. She smiles and
lifts the receiver.*

Brian It's 7am. and this is your early morning obscene telephone
call. You have three minutes to get aroused.

Mrs Clarke, Allison's *mother, enters.*

Allison I'm sorry caller. Security are here to check the bugging
device. Please call later. (*She replaces the receiver.*) Good morning
Mother.

Mrs Clarke Who was that on the phone?

Allison (*smiling*) The Divis Flats heavy breather.

Mrs Clarke Oh really Allison. Can't you be serious about anything!

Allison You know very well who it was, mother. And yes, I'm serious
about a lot of things, but you don't want to know about them.
Particularly at seven o'clock on a Saturday morning. What are you
doing out of bed this early anyway? Is there a bomb scare in our
select suburb?

Mrs Clarke That's not funny, Allison.

Allison No, it's not.

Mrs Clarke Susan phoned last night when you were out.

She left a message for you.

Allison She's emigrating.

Mrs Clarke I do wish you two could be friends.

Allison Mother, it is a legal fact that when Susan married your beloved son, I acquired a sister in law. There is no law says I have to like her.

Mrs Clarke She's such a lovely, likeable girl. A good wife and mother. A considerate daughter-in-law.

Allison A lousy daughter.

Mrs Clarke Susan is very generous to her own mother.

Allison Then this message is not what I suspect it is?

Mrs Clarke Susan can't take Mrs Boyd to . . . that place . . . today.

Allison That place is called Long Kesh. The Maze Prison. and Susan's brother Hughie is one of its most notorious inmates. What's today's excuse for not giving her mother a lift there in the nice new car you bought her for Christmas?

Mrs Clarke Susan has a cold.

Allison In her feet no doubt.

Mrs Clarke She wanted to know if you would give Mrs Boyd a lift, as it's your morning for voluntary work.

Allison Voluntary work? Is that what you tell your friends I do at the camp.

Mrs Clarke Well, it is what you do.

Allison I make tea.

Mrs Clarke Well, there you are then.

Allison It's not like the Women's Institute, mother. It's a drafty hut where the relatives of the prisoners hang around waiting for security clearance before they're bused up the road to the main camp. Voluntary work! Do you know what Susan calls it? Doing my middle class bit. Mingling with the lower orders, the undeserving poor, from behind the safety of a tea urn on a counter. And she's right. That's what galls me. In her own nasty little way, she's right. But she has no right to judge me. Her only brother has been remanded there for over a year, and she has been to see him once.

Mrs Clarke She doesn't know what to say to Hughie.

Allison No. She's married into the middle classes; got herself out of those mean back streets; and his arrest has forced her to look back to what she came from.

Mrs Clarke She is not responsible for her brother.

Allison She could care a little more about her mother.

Mrs Clarke You're very hard on poor Susan. I think she's coped wonderfully well under the circumstances. It hasn't been easy for her.

Allison It hasn't been easy for her mother either. Have you any idea what it's like for a quiet, gentle little woman like Mrs Boyd to go to that place alone. To face the searches, the questions, the police guard while you try to talk to your only son?

The phone rings again. **Allison** *lifts the receiver.*

Brian I've thought it over, and I've decided to give you a second chance.

Allison To do what?

Brian To tell me how madly you love me.

Allison Love you? Are you mad? You're a working class Catholic.

Brian I'm a very sexy working class Catholic.

Allison Are you going to make an honest woman of me?

Brian Not until you've told me why you hung up on me.

Allison I got distracted by a message from your cousin, the lovely Susan.

Brian Ah, let me guess . . . She's broken her leg and can't drive to Long Kesh today.

Allison Congratulations contestant. You have won first prize in our 'spot-the-lame-excuse' competition.

Brian No stamina, these middle class prods.

Allison Common Catholics are not permitted to speak ill of the Protestant Ascendancy. It's written into The Constitution.

Brian I didn't know that.

Allison It's in the small print. Now, if I were your wife, I couldn't be called to give evidence against you.

Brian If you were my wife, I'd be part of the Protestant Ascendancy.

Allison Well, if you don't want to become a handsome prince, I'll become a frog. I'm not proud.

Brian You never give up, do you.

Allison Never.

Brian If I let you take me out tonight and get me drunk, will you promise not to take advantage of me.

Allison No.

Brian Nine o'clock?

Allison Nine o'clock.

Brian And will you drive Aunt Isa to the camp to see Hughie?

Allison You know I will.

Brian You know, you're not a bad sort . . . for a Protestant.

Allison I love you.

Brian I know.

Allison *replaces the receiver.*

Mrs Clarke Allison . . .

Allison Not now mother. I have to pick up Mrs Boyd and be at the camp by nine.

Mrs Clarke We have got to have a serious talk sometime soon.

Allison Mother, I am over eighteen and I don't need your permission to do anything.

Mrs Clarke You're not serious about this person, are you?

Allison He has a name, mother. Brian Rafferty. He was here only last week. Remember? Eye-patch. Wooden leg. Parrot on his shoulder.

Mrs Clarke He is most unsuitable.

Allison Why?

Mrs Clarke His background . . .

Allison Is exactly the same as Susan's.

Mrs Clarke His family . . .

Allison Is Catholic, and Susan's is not.

Mrs Clarke His brother is a terrorist.

Allison So is Susan's. Or are there terrorists and terrorists, mother? Theirs and ours?

Mrs Clarke Henry is very concerned about this whole affair.

Allison You are not to discuss my affairs with Uncle Henry.

Mrs Clarke A marriage of this sort could have detrimental effect on your Uncle Henry's career.

Allison Mother, if I thought for one moment that me marrying a Catholic could put a stop to Uncle Henry's career, as you call it, I'd marry the first Catholic who'd have me.

Mrs Clarke My brother is a very important man.

Allison Your brother is a well-bred gangster.

Mrs Clarke He says he will not permit this.

Allison How's he planning to stop us?

Mrs Clarke *looks uncomfortable and moves away.*

Allison Mother! What did he say!

The Rafferty House.

Brian *returns to help* **Marie** *pack* **Joe** *'s parcel.*

Marie And how is little miss wonderful this morning? Nobody's put a bullet through her head yet, I take it?

Brian Marie, some day that mouth of yours is going to get your nose broke.

Mrs Clarke Or better still, maybe somebody'll put a bullet through her Uncle Henry's head.

Brian Stop it, Marie.

Marie I don't understand how you can go about with the likes of her. It's her kind are responsible for our Joe being where he is. You should be concentrating on getting him out of that place. Not knocking about with well to do Prods. from up the Malone Road.

Brian I'm sorry to be such a disappointment to you and your friends, Marie. I tell you what. As soon as I get my Rambo Outfit back from the cleaners, I'll scale the wire and carry our Joe out on my back.

Mrs Clarke Long Kesh is no joking matter.

Brian No it's not. (*Pause.*) Wouldn't it be a laugh though, if that camp was what united the Irish, once and for all.

Marie What are you blethering on about now.

Brian Where else do you know of in Northern Ireland where the Prods. and the Fenians meet on common ground?

Marie Let's all say a wee prayer together? Our church this week, their church next week?

Brian I said Prods. and Fenians, Marie. Not well-meaning moderates.

Marie The camp, like the country, is segregated.

Brian I'm not talking about the prisoners. I'm talking about their families. Drinking tea in the waiting area. Together. Standing in line checking in food parcels. Together. Sharing the same bus to the main camp to visit their sons, fathers, husbands, brothers, lovers. Together.

Marie They don't visit together. They go their separate ways to segregated blocks. Prods to the right. Fenians to the left.

Brian But before that they've sat together and talked. Without fighting. Which is more than can be said about their so-called political leaders. Maybe we should put all the Politicians on the Long Kesh bus, and drive them round and round the camp till they've reached an agreement.

Marie There'll be no agreement here as long as there are H Blocks and men on the blanket.

Brian There are Protestants in the prison as well, Marie.

Marie One or two.

Brian Well the pair of them must have a hell of a lot of visitors, that's all I can say.

Marie All right. All right. So there are Protestants in jail too. So what!

Brian So, where else in Northern Ireland can a Provie wife and a U.D.A. wife take a long look at each other and realise that they're both on board the same sinking ship. Common ground. Common Enemy. And there's nothing like a common enemy for resolving a family feud.

Marie It's too late Brian.

Brian It's never too late to hold out your hand.

Marie You're a dreamer. They'd tie your hands behind your back and shoot you. You finish Joe's box. I'll take mum up a cup of tea.

Brian How is she the day?

Marie Same as usual. Full of life and hope. Chatting away, ten to the dozen.

Brian Don't, Marie.

Marie What do you want me to say! You know how she is! You still believe there'll be a miraculous cure don't you. That some morning she won't be lying in that bed staring blankly at the cracks in the ceiling. How is she the day! She's the same as she's been every day since some Protestant hero crept up behind daddy and fired a bullet into the back of his head.

Brian We don't know who killed him, Marie.

Marie Maybe he shot himself.

The Clarke House.

Allison's *father,* **Mr Clarke** *comes in.*

Mr Clarke What are you doing up at this hour on a Saturday morning?

Allison It's my Saturday for making tea at the Maze. What's your excuse?

Mr Clarke Didn't your mother tell you? We're going to Enniskillen for the weekend. Your Uncle Henry is having one of his do's.

Allison Oh daddy. Why don't you just refuse to go.

Mr Clarke Your mother would sulk for a fortnight. Besides, I like to keep on friendly terms with Henry. If we ever get our parliament back, he could be our new leader.

Allison God forbid.

Mr Clarke He was born with the gift of the gab.

Allison I wonder how many people have died as a result of his clever speeches.

Mr Clarke What's the matter, love?

Allison It's been one of those mornings. Susan's leaving her mother to face the camp alone again. And mother's been going on about Brian. How unsuitable he is, wrong class, wrong religion . . . do you disapprove of Brian?

Mr Clarke If I let you into a family secret will you promise never to tell your mother that I told you? My grandmother was Catholic. A native Irish speaker from Donegal. I think your mother is very worried that it might be a hereditary complaint coming out in you.

Allison Dad, I get enough jokes from Brian. Don't you start.

Mr Clarke No joke love. Just the unspoken truth. It was an important clause in the marriage contract that it should never be mentioned. I think over the years, your mother has convinced herself that my grandmother was a senile old woman who only imagined she was born a Catholic.

Allison You wouldn't object then, if I married Brian?

Mr Clarke You're over eighteen.

Allison That's not an answer.

Mr Clarke It would . . . worry me.

Allison Why?

Mr Clarke I don't care one way or the other about religion. You know that. I'm all for people leaving each other alone. But unfortunately, there are too many people here who do care. I don't want to see you getting hurt.

Allison Bigoted opinions don't bother me.

Mr Clarke It's not what they'd say, Allison. It's what they might do.

Allison Oh come on daddy. Brian and I aren't that important.

Mr Clarke Whether you like it or not, you are the niece of a loyalist politician. You marry a Catholic and it will be headline news. Especially when word gets out that the groom's brother is Joe Rafferty.

Allison You do disapprove.

Mr Clarke No. I like Brian. He's witty, articulate, good education, good job. In any other time and place the perfect son-in-law. But not here Allison, not now.

Allison I was prepared for objections from every side. His family. Mother's family. All comers. But not you. Not my nice easy-going, middle of-the-road dad.

Mr Clarke Listen to me, love.

Allison Don't waste your breath trying to talk me out of it.

Mr Clarke Let me tell you another family story from way back. Your grandfather, my father, had a stroke and I found myself suddenly in charge of the factory. There was . . . an arrangement . . . about the workforce. There wasn't a Catholic employed in the place. Protestants all. From the managing director to the old man who swept the floors. I'd always known about it, but I'd never really given it much thought until I became the boss. I'd been away from Ireland a lot. Educated in England. Travels abroad. I considered myself a liberal thinker. I was naive enough to believe that good intentions could change the world. Your Brian is like that. I was wrong, of course. When word got around the factory that I'd shortlisted a Catholic woman for canteen manageress, I received a delegation from the men. The message was very clear. Don't even consider it or we shut down the plant. The same day, I was summoned to my father's bedside. He was propped up with pillows. Half paralysed. But *his* message was also very clear. One more stunt like that and he'd bring my cousin George in as head of the family business. Whatever damn fool ideas I'd picked up in Oxford, I could forget them.

Allison So you forget them.

Mr Clarke I'd like to claim a great crisis of conscience. But I'm afraid I can't. I was an indolent young man. I had a sports car. An expensive social life, here and abroad. All paid for by my father's factory with its loyal Protestant workforce. I wasn't about to rock that gilt-edged boat for lost causes.

Allison You've never deliberately harmed anyone. Not like Uncle Henry.

Mr Clarke I've never gone out of my way to help anyone either. What is happening now in this country has come about not just because of greedy politicians, but because of people like me. Influential people of my generation who knew it was wrong, but did nothing to change it. The sins of the fathers shall be visited on the children. As my father was threatening me in his sick slurred voice, the face of his beautiful Catholic mother was smiling down at us from over the fireplace in his bedroom. He loved her. But when she was dying and asked for a Priest, in Irish, he pretended not to understand what she was saying. Perhaps the child of a mixed marriage has more to prove than most.

Allison Is that what's worrying you? My children?

Mr Clarke What's really worrying me is that you might not live long enough to have any children.

Pause.

Allison I'm going to marry him.

Mr Clarke When?

Allison As soon as he'll have me. He keeps turning me down you see. Says he can't afford to keep me in the style to which I am accustomed.

The Rafferty house.

Sounds of coughing offstage. **Brian** *grins as* **Bernie Cassidy** *enters.*

Brian Morning Bernie. You're coughing better. I thought the doctor said you were to give up the fegs.

Bernie Ach bugger him. You're a long time dead. Have you any spare seats in the mini-bus the day?

Brian I thought your Peter got out last week?

Bernie Oh he did. But I'm takin' a parcel down for young Declan Reilly. His mother's in bed with her stomach again.

Brian I think you like going down to The Maze, Bernie.

Bernie When you've been goin' down twice a week for two years, it's hard to give up. Like the fegs.

Brian And how's your Peter coping with the big wide world?

Bernie Oh he's alright. I'm the one that's sufferin'.

Brian Ah now, two years is a long time Mrs Cassidy. They say it can make an animal of a man.

Bernie You're an awful wee boy Brian. I'm not talkin' about that. Jeesus, I wish I was.

Brian Well, what are you talking about then?

Bernie Well to tell you the truth Brian, I never had such a good time in all my married life as I did when he got lifted. 'Ach Mrs Cassidy, sorry to hear about your wee bit of trouble. Can I get you a drink?' Jeesus it was stickin' out, while it lasted. But you see now he's out? My tongue could be hangin' out to my knees for all the notice anybody takes of me. Nobody's bought me as much as a packet of crisps in the last fortnight. You see when your man's put away? You're a star. You see when he gets out? You're nuthin'.

Marie *enters.*

Marie Everybody's in the mini-bus, ready to go.
Hello Bernie.

Bernie Hello Marie, love.

Brian Well, I'd better get my driving gloves on, for the mystery tour.

Bernie Any prizes for guessin' where we're goin'?

Brian First prize, one week in Long Kesh. Second prize?

Bernie Two weeks in Long Kesh.

Brian Third prize, indefinite internment.

Bernie God, you're a tonic Brian. Here, these fegs'll never see me through the day. Hang on. I'll not be a minute. Don't be goin' .without me now.

Bernie *rushes out. There is a slight pause.*

Marie Brian . . . I'm sorry about this morning. I just get angry. Every morning I go into her room and I think, this is the day it's going to be all right. She's going to be back to normal. Sitting up. Smiling. But she never is.

Brian Allison's not responsible for what happened to mum.

Marie I said I'm sorry.

Brian You know, when you take off your black beret and dark glasses and stop mouthing political slogans, you're not a bad looking girl at all. If you weren't my sister, I'd ask you out.

Marie Are you ever serious about anything?

Brian Only the increasing shortage of good pubs since the bombing started.

Spotlight on the **Comedian**.

Comedian Did you hear about the Irishman who was arrested for shoplifting? He lifted the shop three feet off the ground. What happened to the Irishman who tried to blow up a bus? He burned his lips on the exhaust pipe.

A Belfast businessman rushed into an insurance office and asked. 'How much to insure my car against fire?' 'Thirty pounds sir', said the clerk, 'but for only ten pounds extra you can insure it against theft as well.'

'Don't talk daft', said the businessman, 'Sure, who'd want to steal a burning car.'

Irishman Clothing permitted for remand prisoners.
1 pair of shoes. Trainers are allowed but no shoes with steel tips.
3 pairs of socks. 3 sets of underwear.
3 pair of trousers – jeans accepted. 3 shirts.
No pure white, black, blue or green colours are allowed for any article of clothing.

Comedian What do you do if an Irishman throws a pin at you? Run like hell. He's probably got a grenade between his teeth.

Did you hear the one about the Irishman whose library was burned down? Both books were destroyed. And worse still, one of them hadn't even been coloured in.

Belfast City Hall was bombed and the Lord Mayor phoned the Fire Brigade. 'Have you taken any steps to quench the blaze?' asked the fire chief. 'My staff are pouring buckets of water on it' said the Lord Mayor.

'Well, there's no point in us coming over', said the fire chief, 'sure that's all we'd be doing too.'

Irishman 2 pairs of pyjamas. Only type with elastic waistbands are acceptable.

3 jumpers. No slogans allowed except manufacturers trade mark – for example, Adidas.

Comedian Mick and Paddy were planting a bomb, and Mick said, 'Hey Paddy, hold that wire'. And then Mick put his fingers in his ears. A couple of minutes later he took them out again and said, 'What happened?' 'Nothing', said Paddy. 'Thank God for that', said Mick, 'it must be the other wire that triggers the explosion'. He must be the same Irishman who read a poster that said: Man wanted for bombing and murder. So he went in and applied for the job.

What's the fastest sport in the world? Pass the parcel in an Irish pub.

An Irish pub was bombed and the landlord rushed to the nearest

telephone box. 'Hello, is that 999?' 'No, this is 998'. 'Well, would
you ever nip next door and tell tham me pub's on fire?'
He was the same barmen who thought that Vat 69 was the Pope's
telephone number.

Irishman One outdoor jacket. Not hooded.
One indoor jacket. Not leather or imitation leather.
Bomber jackets not allowed.

The Maze Prison. 9a.m.
Brian *and* **Marie** *in the waiting room*
Allison *enters with their Aunt* **Mrs Boyd.**

Brian Hello Aunt Isa.

Mrs Boyd Hello Brian love. (*Slight pause.*) Hello Marie.

Marie *takes* **Joe** *'s parcel from* **Brian**.

Marie I'll go and sign our Joe's parcel in.

She exits. There is a small awkward silence.

Brian Give me Hughie's parcel, Allison. I'll sign it in. You get the
tea urn going.

Allison *hands him* **Hughie** *'s parcel and leaves* **Brian** *alone with* **Mrs
Boyd**.

Brian I'm sorry about Marie.

Mrs Boyd She was very close to your dad.

Brian We all were. Including you. He used to tease my mother, you
know. Say it was a close thing whether he married her or you.
(*Hurriedly, because* **Mrs Boyd** *looks as if she might cry.*) Here, these are
for Hughie. I called round with them yesterday, but you weren't in.

He puts a packet of cigarettes into **Hughie** *'s box.* **Allison** *returns.*

Allison Tea'll be ready in about five minutes.

Brian I'll go and check the parcel in. You haven't hidden a file or
anything in the baps, have you Aunt Isa?

Mrs Boyd I'll do it, Brian.

Brian No, I want to do it. Joe Rafferty's brother checking in a
parcel for the Protestant compound? The computer'll do its nut.

He exits.

Mrs Boyd He's good boy. Always was. I remember him when he was a little child. Always laughing.

Allison He still is.

Mrs Boyd Are the two of you still going out together?

Allison Yes. You're not going to give me a lecture, are you? I get enough of those from my mother.

Mrs Boyd Do you go to his house?

Allison Not very often.

Mrs Boyd We used to go there every Sunday for our tea. Me and Hughie and Susan. After my Sammy died. It all seems such a long time ago.

Allison Why don't you go and see her. She just lies in her bed, day in day out, staring, seeing God knows what.

Mrs Boyd I remember the day she married Paddy Rafferty. Lovely she was. Dark blue suit. Kid gloves. I bought her the gloves. Mother and father refused to go to the wedding. But we went. Sammy and me. My Sammy gave her away. Paddy was his mate. They were in The Union together. Thought they were going to change the world. Afterwards, in the pub, we all promised one another that no matter what happened, we'd always be close. Nothing in the world would ever drive us apart. We're twins, Molly and me. Did you know that? She was the oldest by half an hour. I used to be jealous of that when we were kids.

Allison Let me take you to see her.

Mrs Boyd Then the troubles broke out, and Paddy got shot. I suppose they'd have shot my Sammy too, if the cancer hadn't got him first.

Allison She might respond to you.

Mrs Boyd We went to Paddy's funeral, our Hughie and Susan and me. There was a big crowd outside in the street. A woman spat in my face. I went a few times after that. And then the threatening letters came. I was scared. There were a lot of sectarian murders that year. Anyway, our Molly didn't know me anymore. Didn't know anybody. So I stopped going. One night our Hughie got beaten up on his way from from the pictures. He said Joe was there. Did nothing to help him. I couldn't believe it. Next thing I hear the police are looking for Joe in connection with an explosion in a pub in Belfast. Two people were killed. Then our Hughie took to stopping out late. By this time, Susan was married to your brother John, and the baby was on the way. I didn't want to worry her. I used to sit on my own, waiting for Hughie to come home. But when he did come back, in the small hours of the morning, I never could ask him where he'd been. What he'd been doing. I suppose I knew. Didn't want to know. And now he's locked up here. And so is Joe. They were like brothers when they were kids. We used to share a house near the sea, every summer. I don't understand why all this has happened to us. Paddy and Sammy must be turning over in their graves.

Allison Brian still keeps in touch with you.

Mrs Boyd Allison, I want you to tell Brian to stop visiting me. There's been talk in the street. I've tried to tell him, but he won't listen. Just laughs, makes jokes, tells me not to be so daft. I care about that wee boy like he was one of my own. I don't want to see him getting hurt.

Allison Why would anyone want to hurt Brian. He's the most gentle, caring man I've ever known.

Mrs Boyd So was his father. (*Pause.*) You'd better go and help with the tea. They'll be wondering what's keeping you.

Allison They've got more helpers than they need today. So, I'm going in to the camp with you to visit Hughie. Your Susan says I've no idea what it's like in there. Maybe it's about time I found out.

Spotlight on the **Comedian**.

Comedian Of course two thirds of the Irish people don't know what the other half is doing. Maggie Thatcher was in Rome to talk to the Pope about the Northern Ireland situation, and she discovered that the Pope had a direct line to God. So she asked His Holiness if she could make the call. 'Certainly', said the Holy Father, 'but it's very expensive. About fifty million lire'. Now Maggie had used up all her traveller's cheques, so she couldn't afford to make the call. But next time she was in Belfast she noticed that Ian Paisley *also* had a hot line to God, so she asked *him* if she could make the call.
'Certainly', said Big Ian. 'It'll cost you 10p'. '10p!' said Maggie. 'Do you know that it costs fifty million lire to phone God from the Vatican? Why is it so cheap from Belfast?' 'Because it's a local call,' said Ian.

Of course it was dear old Uncle Ian who said that all Irish people should link hands and go their separate ways.

Grow your own dope. Plant an Irishman. (*He reads from a copy of the Sun.*) Have you seen the paper today? It says here that the Irish attempt on Everest has failed. They've run out of scaffolding. Mind you, it also says that Mrs Murphy has moved her house two feet forward to take up the slack in her clothes-line. And Mr Murphy's not much better. He was given two weeks to live. So he said, 'I'll take one in June and one in September.'

Allo! The Irish daredevil Evil O'Kneivel has failed in his attempt to jump over twenty three motor bikes in a bus.

He puts the paper aside.

What happened to the Irish jellyfish? It set! How do you tell an Irish pirate? He wears an eye-patch over both eyes.

And what about the Irish Godfather who made an offer he couldn't remember?

The Protestant compound.

Allison, **Mrs Boyd** *and* **Hughie**.

Mrs Boyd There's a lovely bit of cooked ham in your parcel, son. Ellie Wilson sent it.

Hughie (*To* **Allison**) Ellie Wilson nicks it out of Jamieson's shop.

Mrs Boyd She does not, Hughie.

Hughie She does so. (*To* **Allison**.) Ever since oul Johnnie Jamieson refused to make a decent contribution to the Prisoner's Defence Fund, Ellie's been feeding half the inmates here at Johnnie's expense, without him knowing it.(*Pause.*) Thanks for bringing my mother down Allison. You're more like a daughter to her than our Susan ever was.

Allison Brian sent you some cigarettes.

Hughie Allison, I have to talk to you. Now listen, and listen carefully. There's been a lot of talk in here about you and Brian. Not very nice talk.

Mrs Boyd There's been talk in the street too.

Hughie I know. The word is that Brian's not just visiting his Aunt. That he's in our street to collect information for the other side.

Allison You can't believe that.

Hughie I've known Brian all his life. I know there's no harm in him. But they don't know that.

Allison Well you tell them.

Hughie Why should they believe me? I'm his cousin. And now they've found out that he's going about with you. They think he's a spy, sent to get information about your Uncle Henry.

Allison That's the daftest thing I ever heard.

Hughie Not half as daft as him ignoring the danger he's in. Now I can't stop him going out with you, but you're to tell him, and make sure he heeds, that he's not to visit my mother any more. Brian thinks he can joke his way out of anything. But his sense of humour won't save him if some joker decides to put a bullet through his head.

Spotlight on the **Comedian**.

Comedian Sean was confessing his sins to Father O'Reilly. 'Forgive me Father, for I have sinned. I've been to bed with a Protestant.'
'What Protestant!' roared the Priest.
'Oh, I couldn't tell you that, Father', said Sean, 'It wouldn't be honourable.'
'Was it Margaret Stewart from the fruit shop?'
'No, Father.'
'Was it that schoolteacher, Fiona Wilson?'
'No, Father.'
'Well, who was it then!'
'Forgive me, Father. But a gentleman never reveals a lady's name. Even if she is a Protestant.'
'You'll either confess her name, or do a penance of ten Hail Marys,' threatened the Priest.
'I'll do the penance Father,' said Sean, and went outside to meet his friend Paddy.
'How did you get on?' asked Paddy.
'Great,' said Sean. 'Ten Hail Marys, and a couple of dead certs for the night.'

The Catholic compound.

Brian, **Marie** *and* **Joe** .

Brian Allison's not really a Prod. you know. Rumour has it that her oul granda was Jewish on his mother's side.

Joe The time for silly jokes is over, Brian. Stop seeing her. The boys don't like it.

Brian The boys aren't gettin' it. Aw come on, Joe. It wasn't one of my best, but you might manage a little smile. You used to have a great sense of fun, in the old days.

Joe The old days are over.

Marie Her uncle is a leading loyalist politician, committed to Protestant supremacy in The North.

Brian Is that a quote from the Sein Fein Handbook, Marie? Henry Sinclair doesn't give a damn about religion. What he worships is money and power. Allison can't stand him.

Joe We've only your word for that, Brian.

Brian What's with the 'we', Joe? Do I take it, if somebody has a pot-shot at me some dark night, that you might be behind it?

Joe Don't talk stupid Brian. I'm your brother, and I've been told to tell you.

Brian So now you've told me.

Joe Will you stop seeing her?

Brian No.

Joe You don't understand.

Brian Oh, I understand all right.

Joe Listen to me.

Brian No. You listen to me. You've been here so long Joe, that you think nothing else matters but The Troubles. Well you're wrong. Outside of here, in the real world, fellas and girls still go out together. To the pubs, the parks, the pictures. Normal life goes on Joe, outside these wire fences. And that's all Allison and me are. Just a couple of normal people who fancy each other rotten . . .

Joe Listen!

Brian No! You listen! I'm going to marry Allison Clarke. And some cowboy threatening to blow my head off is not going to stop me.

Joe If you care about her that much, then give her up. It's not your head they're threatening to blow off. It's hers.

Spotlight on the **Comedian**

Comedian It's not widely known that God at first intended to have

his Only Son born in Belfast. But he couldn't find Three Wise Men.
Or a virgin.

What do you call a pregnant Irishwoman? A dope carrier.

They're all thick, the Irish. That's why it says 'Open other end' on
the bottom of all the Guinness bottles.

Paddy was having a pint one night, when Mick came into the pub
with a big sack over his shoulder. 'What's in the sack?' asked Paddy.
'Ducks,' said Mick. Now Paddy was a bit of a punter, so he said to
Mick, 'If I guess how many ducks there are in the sack, will you give
me one of them?' 'If you guess how many ducks there are in the
bag,' said Mick, 'I'll give you both of them.'

'Eh . . . five,' said Paddy.

Later that evening.

Brian *and* **Allison** *in a lounge bar in Belfast.*

Brian I hate plastic pubs. And piped music.

Allison Well what do you fancy? A sing-song at the U.D.A. club? Or
you could take me to a real Irish pub up The Falls. I hear the
music's great.

Brian Aye, and the drink's half the price. I'm not surprised they're
so short on customers here.

Allison It's early yet. The place'll fill up later.

Brian It's nearly half past nine.

Allison You've got your watch back.

Brian One of the kids came up to me in school yesterday. 'Here's
your watch, sir,' he said. 'And my big brother says to tell you if you
ever have anything else pinched, just let him know.' How do I
explain to a nine year old boy who's never known anything better,
that I don't want his big brother threatening to knee-cap some
other little boy, if he doesn't give the teacher back his watch? How
does anybody explain anything about law and order and individual
rights to a child whose earliest memory is of his mother screaming
when armed soldiers broke down the door at four o'clock in the
morning, and dragged his father out of bed and into a landrover.
Why should that child respect the law that allows the army and the
police to terrorize in the name of catching terrorists. His father was
interrogated for two days simply because he was the secretary of a
Gaelic Football team, and made regular trips across the border to
arrange matches in The South. And after his release when he tried

to sue them for wrongful arrest, they harrassed his wife and children until he dropped the case. Now his oldest son organizes big league games for the I.R.A. and the nine year old can't wait until he's old enough to shoot a man in uniform. The British never learn, do they? Men with guns create other men with guns. And that child learned very early on that the men with the most guns win. And he's right.

Allison What's up doc?

Brian I have to have a serious talk with you, Allison.

Allison God, it must be the time of year. Everybody wants to talk seriously to me these days. You haven't finally made up your mind to propose to me, have you? My stars today said I would find myself in an unusual situation.

Brian I think maybe we should . . . ease off for a while . . . not see so much of each other . . . give ourselves time to think.

Allison Go on.

Brian I don't want to settle down. The world's full of women I've never met.

Allison It won't work Brian.

Brian Oh I don't know. If I started tomorrow, I might work my way round half of them anyway, before I'm too old to enjoy it.

Allison Somebody's threatened me. They have, haven't they?

Brian I'm not in love with you.

Allison Look at me when you're talking to me.

Brian There's a group of hard men in Long Kesh who think that you're spying for Uncle Henry.

Allison Funny you should mention that. There's a second group of hard men in Long Kesh who think that you're spying for the first group.

They stare at each other for a moment and then laugh.

Brian You know, if we get shot, we won't even have the satisfaction of knowing who pulled the trigger.

Allison Don't!

Brian Joke, love.

Allison Sometimes I think it's all a very sick joke and we're destined to die laughing. A great life we'd have together. Drawing the curtains before dark. Jumping every time a car stops outside the house.

Brian We could always emigrate. There must be more Irishmen than kangaroos in Australia by now.

Allison I don't want to live in Australia. I want to live here. I want rain in the summer and snow at Easter. I want grey skies and green grass. I want a baby. I want you.

Brian Then we'll stay and prove them all wrong. We'll open the curtains and the front door. And we'll laugh. Show the world that it's all just a silly Irish joke.

Allison Are you asking me to marry you?

Brian Will you, Allison Clarke, promise to have a baby a year and bring them all up to be good little Catholics, and give them ethnic names like Maraid, Sinea, Fergus and Finbar?

Allison Will you, Brian Rafferty, promise to wear an orange sash on the twelfth of July, and beat a big drum in a kick-the-Pope band?

Brian You know something? When you and me get together, Ulster will never know what hit it. We'll be on the Gloria Hunniford show. Co-founders of the Apathetic Party for people who just don't want to know. We won't have a manifesto.

Allison We'll be too apathetic to write one.

Brian We won't have any members.

Allison They'll be too apathetic to join.

Brian We won't have a cause.

Allison Apathetic people don't have causes.

Brian They tell great jokes though.

Allison I love you.

Brian I know.

Allison My parents are away for the weekend.

Brian Well, what are we doing sitting here, when we could be lying in a big Protestant ascendancy bed up the Malone road?

Allison If we do that, you might have to marry me.

Brian And would you?

Allison I might. If you ask me again in the morning.

Spotlight on the **Comedian**.

Comedian How do you recognize the bride and groom at an Irish wedding? She's the one in the white wellies. He's the one in the flared wellies.
Did you hear about the girl who wanted to marry an Irishman, but her parents refused to give their consent. So the lovers decided to commit suicide by jumping off the Lagan Bridge. The girl hit the water alright. But the Irishman got lost on the way down.
What do you call an Irishman who marries a gorilla? A social climber.

Brian I love you.

Allison I know.

They exit, arms around each other.

The **Irishman** *walks on and reads a news bulletin.*

Irishman The two bodies discovered early this morning near the Cave Hill on the outskirts of Belfast, have been identified as twenty-five year-old Allison Clarke and twenty-nine year-old Brian Rafferty.
Miss Clarke was the niece of the Unionist politician Mr Henry Sinclair, who today claimed that the I.R.A. were responsible, and called on the Secretary of State for Northern Ireland to order more troops into the province for the protection of its British citizens.
However, a police spokesman said today that Brian Rafferty comes from a family with known Republican sympathies. His brother Joseph is serving a life sentence in the Maze Prison for terrorist offences including bombing and murder. Police say that they are keeping an open mind as to the identity of the killers, and have appealed for information. The bodies were discovered at 6.00 a.m. by an army patrol . . .

Comedian It was reported in the American newspapers today that there was a Belfast type shooting in Chicago.
'Isn't it funny,' said the Irishman, who was reading the death notices in the Belfast Telegraph, 'how people always seem to die in alphabetical order.'
Did you hear about the Irishman standing in front of the firing squad, who was asked if he'd like a last cigarette? 'No thanks,' he

said, 'I'm trying to give them up.'
An Irishman and an Irish girl were pushed off the top of the Cave
Hill. Who hit the ground first? Who cares, so long as they're both
Irish.
How do you save an Irishman from dying? You don't know? Good.

The **Irishman** *tears the news bulletin into shreds.*

Comedian Hallo Paddy. You still here? (*He walks to the* **Irishman**.)
Have you heard the Irish knock knock joke? You haven't? Right,
you start.

Irishman (*expressionlessly*) Knock. Knock.

Comedian Who's there?

He laughs and begins to walk away.

Irishman (*quietly*) What do you call an Irishman with a machine
gun?

Comedian I don't know, Paddy. What *do* you call an Irishman with
a machine gun?

Irishman (*wearily*) You call him sir.

Blackout.